The Great Drama of Jesus

The Great Drama of Jesus

a life of CHRIST for teens who want to be challenged

by Rev. Victor Galeone

PROW

1600 W. Park Avenue   Libertyville, Illinois 60048

Nihil Obstat: Monsignor Carroll Satterfield

Imprimatur:† Archbishop William D. Borders
Archbishop of Baltimore

March 29, 1979

ISBN 0-913382-31-0

Dedication

"To Mary,
the Immaculata,
the Mother of all youth
who strive to imitate Jesus."

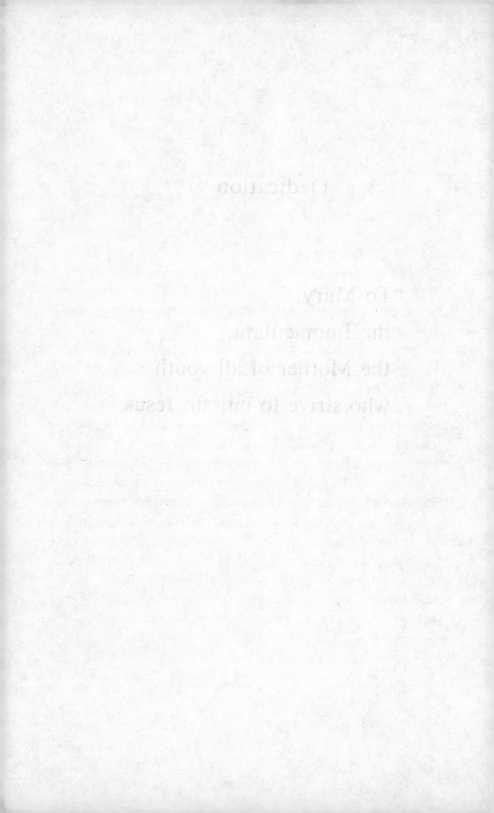

Introduction

During the past several years, I have become acutely aware of the religious illiteracy surrounding our youth. But I do not find fault with them; for they have been subjected to a superficial treatment of doctrine and an exaggerated emphasis on personal development and experience. Still, they continue to thirst for the truth — a thirst which can be quenched only with the strong wine of the pure Gospel message, not with some diluted version that even an agnostic can accept.

To remedy this sad situation was the underlying factor that prompted the present work. Using fifty short scenes from the life of Christ as a springboard for discussion, I have attempted to present a clear and concise picture of what the Church teaches in matters doctrinal and moral. In such a presentation, of necessity, I had to sacrifice the benefit of an orderly arrangement of doctrine. Nevertheless, I hope that my approach, however unsystematic it may seem, will convey to the young the authentic richness of our Catholic faith against the backdrop of the greatest life ever lived.

The instructor may wish to involve the students even more in Jesus' life by assigning them various parts to be "dramatized" in class. However, my objective is not to entertain, but to challenge. Yes, I want to challenge the average high school student to begin to share more fully in our divine birthright — eternal life, which consists "in knowing the Father, the only true God, and the one He sent, Jesus Christ" (Jn. 17:3).

Contents

CONFLICT

DEFEAT

Prologue

God's Word never had a beginning.

He had always been in God's presence,
for His nature was the same as God's.
It was through this Word that everything was created.

Yes, every single creature owes its existence to Him.

Then, when the proper time came,
God's Word took our mortal nature,
was born here on earth like one of us,
and lived right in our midst.

But even though He had created the world,
the world did not recognize Him.

He came to the very people chosen to welcome Him,
but they refused to accept Him.

To everyone who did accept Him
He gave the privilege of becoming adopted children of God.

Yes, some of us have actually seen His glory —
the glory of God's only Son — the Word —
conceived in the Father's mind from all eternity.

No one has ever seen God.
His only Son, Who had always been with the Father,
came to tell us about Him.

—John 1:1-18 *(passim)*

1

Our drama takes place in Palestine, some 2,000 years ago. Our opening scene is set in a rustic dwelling in Nazareth, a small village nestled in the foothills of Galilee. MARY, a girl of 16, is grinding barley. Enter GABRIEL, an angel.

Lk 1:26-38

GABRIEL   Hail, fountain of grace!
          The Lord is with you!

MARY   (*aside, startled*) ". . . fountain of grace"?
          What can that possibly mean?

GABRIEL   Do not be afraid, Mary.
          I am Gabriel,
          sent by God to bring you this marvelous news.
          Listen! You are going to have a child,
          and you are to name him Jesus.
          He will be called Son of the Most High.
          The Lord will set him on the throne
          of his predecessor David.
          He will rule the House of Israel forever,
          and his royal power will never have an end.

MARY   How can that be?
          I'm to remain a virgin.

GABRIEL   God's Holy Spirit will rest on you
          and His mighty power will envelop you.
          And so they'll call your son the holy Son of God.
          What's more, your relative Elizabeth,
          though up in years, has also conceived a child.
          The very one they used to call " barren"
          will be giving birth within three months.
          For nothing is impossible with God.

The very god they used to call . . . Horror!
. . . be gentle here, within stood many such . . .
. . . nothing is more than still God.

MARY	Let everything happen as you described.
	My only wish is to serve the Lord.

☆　　☆　　☆

CHORUS	*Listen, O House of David!*
	The Lord Himself will give you a sign:
	Behold! The Virgin is with child,
	she will give birth to a son,
	and she will name him EMMANUEL — God-With-Us!

— Isaiah 7:14

BORN OF THE VIRGIN MARY

"How can that be, since I don't know man?" (Lk 1:34)
In biblical language that means:
". . . since I don't have marital relations."
Mary's answer poses a problem:
Gabriel merely informed her that she was to become a mother,
saying nothing of the child's paternity. (v. 31)
But since Mary was already "engaged to Joseph" (v. 27),
if she had planned to have relations after her wedding,
why would she have objected, "I don't know man"?
Suppose someone offers you a cigarette.
"No thanks, I don't smoke."
Do you mean that you're not smoking just for TODAY?
"Of course not. I mean:
I don't smoke now and I NEVER intend to.
I'm a non-smoker."
This example illustrates what Mary really meant:
"I don't know man now and I NEVER intend to.
I plan to remain a *virgin*."
(We know historically from the Dead Sea scrolls
that around the time of Christ,
certain members of the Essene community at Qumran
bound themselves with vows of virginity.)
Gabriel goes on to reassure Mary:
"The Holy Spirit will descend on you . . .: (v. 35)
("Mary, you will conceive without having relations.
The only father your child will have is God.")

3

☆　　☆　　☆

When you recite the words of the Creed,
". . . born of the Virgin Mary . . ."
you're joining countless Christians of all times
who believed that Mary was *always* a virgin.
"You mean, even after the birth of Jesus?"
Yes, even then she never lost her virginity.
"But what about Jesus' brothers and sisters in Mk 6:3?"
Aramaic (the language Jesus spoke)
has no special word for "cousin, nephew, etc."
The word "brother" can mean "any close male relative."
Compare: Gn 12:5 — Abram is Lot's *uncle.*
　　　　　　Gn 13:8 — Abram said to Lot, "We are *brothers.*"
Besides, if Mary had any other children,
why did Jesus, as He was dying on the cross,
entrust her to the care of the beloved John?
"Woman, there is your son." (Jn 19:26)

4

2 A week later. The house of Zachary in the Judean hills. ELIZABETH, a woman in her 60's, is seated with her husband ZACHARY in the garden. Enter MARY.

Lk 1:5-25; 39-56

MARY   (*calling from a distance*) Elizabeth! — Zachary! — Peace!

ELIZABETH   Mary! Most blessed of all the women in the world! And how blessed is the child within your womb!

MARY   How did you learn that, Elizabeth? Tell me.

ELIZABETH   I no sooner heard your greeting
than the baby trembled in my womb with joy.
Mary, you have been richly blessed for believing
that the Lord would do all that He promised.

MARY   O how my soul glorifies the Lord!
And my heart delights in God my Savior!
For He has looked upon His lowly servant.
Now all future ages will call me blessed.
Ever so powerful, He has filled me with wonders.
How holy is His name!
For those who honor Him His mercy never dies.
His powerful arm has pushed back the proud.
He has toppled mighty rulers
and raised up lowly peasants.
The rich He's made poor,
and the poor He's filled with riches.
He took in Israel as His servant,
recalling the promise He made to our ancestors:
first to Abraham,
and then to all of his descendants.

5

ZACHARY *crosses to* MARY *and pantomimes a greeting.*

MARY   Zachary, what's the matter?
Why aren't you speaking?

ELIZABETH   It happened six months ago — on Temple duty.
They had selected him to offer incense
at the morning sacrifice.
On entering the Holy Place,
he saw an angel of the Lord.
Zachary was terrified,
so the angel told him not to be afraid.
He said that we were going to have a son
and were to name him John.
He's been appointed to prepare our people
to welcome the Messiah.

MARY   How wonderful the Lords' ways are —
that all of this should happen at your age!

ELIZABETH   But Zachary doubted every single word.
So the angel went on to tell him:
"I am Gabriel. I've been sent by God
to bring you this good news.
But for refusing to believe me,
you will lose your voice until the child is born."
— Mary, your journey must have worn you out.
How long will you be staying?

MARY   For three months.
I'll be here to help you until the child arrives.

ELIZABETH   How fortunate I am
to have the Mother of my Lord come to visit me!

CHORUS   *And David said:*
"Who am I to have the ark of the Lord come to me?"
The ark of the Lord remained
in the house of Obed-edom for three months,
and the Lord blesses Obed-edom and his family.
                            — 2 Samuel 6:9,11

6

MOTHER OF GOD

"How have I deserved a visit from the Mother of my LORD?"
Here, Elizabeth is inspired by God. (Lk 1:41)
She is the first to honor Mary with a title
which later Christians would clarify as "Mother of GOD."
Many years ago Nestorius was the bishop of Constantinople.
In 428 he began preaching in his sermons:
"Mary is the mother of Christ but not the mother of God."
The faithful were quick to react; for they sensed
that this opinion would make TWO persons of Christ:
one human, the other divine.
Emperor, bishops, and Pope were informed.
In 431 a council was convoked at Ephesus.
There it was solemnly proclaimed
that Mary is truly the Mother of God.
No one denies that Mary is the mother of Jesus.
She gave Him what every mother gives her child:
a tiny body to which God joins an immortal soul.
Still, a woman is mother not of a *body* but of a *person*.
(How would you react if someone introduced herself:
"Hello. I'm the mother of Jane's body."?)
But in Jesus there is only *one* person — a *divine* person:
"The Word was God . . . and the Word became flesh." (Jn 1:1,14)
And so Mary is truly the Mother of God:
not of God the Father,
not of God the Holy Spirit,
but of God the Son.
Like any mother, she really conceived Him in her womb,
she carried Him there for nine months,
she gave birth to Him,
and she nursed Him at her breast.
To deny that Mary is the Mother of God
is to deny that Jesus is God.

☆   ☆   ☆

Luke 1:43 also shows the evil of ABORTION:
Mary had been carrying her child less than a week. (v. 38,39)
Yet Elizabeth already calls the *embryo* "my Lord" — a person!
So in abortion one terminates not just a pregnancy,
but the life of an innocent *person!*

7

3 Nazareth, three months later. In the carpenter shop — bathed in moonlight — JOSEPH, Mary's fiance, is sitting up on his bed of animal skins.

Mt 1:18-21

JOSEPH (*musing aloud*) How could this have happened?
And after we consecrated our bodies to the Lord!
She must be innocent.
But still — what could have happened?
I don't want to ruin her good name. —
Perhaps I'll break the engagement quietly and —
O Lord, give me light.
Show me what I must do!

(*He lies back and falls asleep. Enter* GABRIEL.)

GABRIEL Joseph! — Joseph!

JOSEPH (*sitting up, startled*) Who's there?

GABRIEL Joseph, son of David,
do not be afraid to take Mary as your wife.
Her child was conceived by Power from on High.
When she has given birth,
you must name the child JESUS,
for he shall SAVE his people from their sins.

☆　　☆　　☆

CHORUS *And Joseph said:*
"My lord has put such confidence in me
that he has given me his all.
He has denied me nothing but you,
for you are his bride."

— *Genesis 39:8,9*

8

THE CARPENTER'S SON

"Mary stayed with Elizabeth about three months . . ." (Lk 1:56)
Shortly after her return to Nazareth,
Joseph noticed Mary's condition.
He knew nothing of the angel's visit.
How then explain the pregnancy?
And what should he do about it?
The Law of Moses was quite explicit:
"If a virgin is engaged to be married,
and another man has relations with her,
you shall take them both out to the town gate,
and stone them to death," (Dt 22:23)
Though mystified by Mary's condition,
Joseph was still convinced of her virtue.
So to protect her from the Law,
he planned to break the engagement privately.
That night, a dream revealed God's designs.
The next day, Joseph advanced the date of the wedding
before gossiping tongues could cast doubts
on the child's paternity.
And so it was that Jesus came to be known as
"the son of the carpenter." (Mt 13:55)

☆　　☆　　☆

Of all the figures that form part
of the inner circle of Jesus' life,
we know the least about St. Joseph.
Not a single word he spoke has been preserved.
Just his unquestioning submission to the Will of God:
"Joseph, get up! Herod is after the child's life!
Take the child and his mother
and escape to Egypt . . ." (Mt 2:13)
If you had been asked to do that, what would you have said?
"Now? In the middle of the night?.
It's cold. Why not wait until morning?"
Instead, we read: "So Joseph got up . . .
and left *that night* for Egypt." (Mt 2:14)

9

What a beautiful lesson!
He exemplifies perfectly what St. James pointed out:
"The one who never offends in word
has a perfect character." (Jm 3:2)

4 The town square in Nazareth, four months later. The WOMEN and MERCHANTS at the market-stalls pause in their bargaining as the TOWN CRIER enters.

Lk 2:1-5

TOWN
CRIER   (*reading from scroll*) "Hear ye! Hear ye!
By solemn decree of Caesar Augustus,
gloriously reigning in Rome,
there is to be a census taken
in every realm and province.
Accordingly, all are to register
in the township of their forebears
before the first of the month next. —
Hear ye! Hear Ye! By solemn decree of . . ."

He continues down the square. JOSEPH *has been listening with* MARY *at his workshop door.*

JOSEPH   ". . . in the township of their forebears . . ."
For me that's Bethlehem. —
But, Mary, how can I leave you in your condition
to go there and register?

MARY   We shall go together, Joseph.
There is still time.
Besides, we have nothing to fear.
The Lord is our strength!

☆   ☆   ☆

CHORUS   *O Bethlehem,*
the smallest town in all of Judah!
Out of you will come the one
who is to rule my people Israel,
whose origin goes back to everlasting days.
— Micah 5:2

11

PROPHECY: THE MESSIAH'S CREDENTIALS

"Doesn't Scripture say that the Messiah
must come from BETHLEHEM
and be descended from David?" (Jn 7:42)
"Yes! But he's from Nazareth, not Bethlehem!"
Thus, the Jews of Jesus' day were divided over Him.
Many wanted to accept Him as their Messiah,
but felt that He did not match the portrait,
which had been painted centuries before
on the canvas of the Old Testament.
There the Divine Artist had sketched a preview,
outlining the traits of the future Messiah:

Abraham's seed (Gn 22:18)	*of David's blood* (2 Sm 7:12)
Virgin-born (Is 7:14)	*in Bethlehem* (Mi 5:2)
betrayed (Zch 11:12)	*a suffering servant* (Is 53:11)
crucified (Ps 22:16)	*cheating death* (Ps 16:10)

Jesus Himself claimed to fulfill Old Testament prophecies:

"Moses wrote of me . . ."(Jn 5:46)
"Today this Scripture has been fulfilled." (Lk 4:21)
"Then he explained all the texts about himself." (Lk 24:27)
Jesus was the only person ever to present Himself
with credentials — written centuries in advance —
that guaranteed His mission from God.
Every "scene" in this book closes with a quote
from one such Old Testament prophecy or related text.

☆　　☆　　☆

JESUS' FAMILY TREE   (See Mt 1:1-16)

B.C.

2000	ABRAHAM	— father of the Jewish race
1900	ISAAC	— born when Abraham was 100
1850	JACOB	— had 12 sons, heads of the 12 tribes
1800	JUDAH	— the other 11 tribes were eliminated
1000	DAVID	— all other clans were eliminated

MARY + JOSEPH — both were of David's lineage

JESUS   "the son of DAVID as to the **flesh**" (Rm 1:3)
"the Son of GOD as to the **Spirit**" (Rm 1:4)

5 The outskirts of Bethlehem, a few weeks later before dawn. In a cave that serves as a stable, MARY is nursing her CHILD of a few hours. JOSEPH crouches on the straw nearby.

Lk 2:6-20

MARY	O Joseph, he's so beautiful!
JOSEPH	But to be born in an animal shelter! — Still — it's better than that open inn-yard. (*Sounds of commotion outside*) Who goes? Speak up!
1st *SHEPHERD*	(*entering*) We're looking for a new-born baby. (*Seeing MARY with the infant, he turns and calls.*) Men! This must be the place!
	(*Enter two more SHEPHERDS.*)
JOSEPH	Just who are you?
1st *SHEPHERD*	Shepherds from the neighboring hills. We were tending our sheep during the third watch, when an angel of the Lord appeared to us . . .
2nd *SHEPHERD*	(*excited, cuts him off*) We cringed like lambs before a wolf, so he told us not to be afraid. "I'm bringing you the greatest news ever announced on earth. This very night in the town of David, your Savior was born — the Messiah you've been waiting for."
3rd *SHEPHERD*	Then he went on to tell us that we'd find him wrapped in swaddling clothes and lying in a manger.

	So we hurried right over to see for ourselves this wonderful thing the Lord . . .
2nd SHEPHERD	(*cut him off*) Wait!! You forgot to tell about the whole army of angels that appeared. They were all singing this beautiful melody: "Glory to God in the highest! And peace to His servants on earth!"
1st SHEPHERD	Our Messiah! The Lord be praised!
3rd SHEPHERD	(*moving in closer*) Imagine that! The Messiah we've been waiting for! Who will ever believe us?

☆　　☆　　☆

CHORUS	*A child is born for us,* *A son is given to us.* *He bears royal authority on His shoulders.* *And this will be His* NAME: *"Wonderful Counsellor",* *"Mighty God",* *"Eternal Father",* *"Prince of Peace".*

— Isaiah 9:6

A.D. — IN THE YEAR OF OUR LORD

"Foxes have holes, birds have nests,
but the Son of Man has nowhere to rest his head." (Mt 8:20)
These words ring true of Jesus right from His birth.
While earthly kings are born in royal splendor.
God's own Son shared a cave with the ox and the ass.
His mother was the poorest of the poor,
His courtiers, rugged shepherds,
His crib, a feeding-trough.
He grew up in a backward village.
His own countrymen made it the butt of their jokes:
"Can anything good come from Nazareth?" (Jn 1:46)
There, until the age of 30, lost in obscurity,
He worked as a carpenter.

Yet one day, that insignificant carpenter
would change the course of all recorded history:
He split it right in two: B.C. and A.D.
As the moving words of "One Solitary Life" put it:
"He never went to college,
He never wrote a book,
He never raised a family,
He never led an army,
He never travelled more than 200 miles
from the place where He was born.
He did none of the things we associate with greatness . . ."
Yet those who did accomplish great things
now depend on Him for their position in time:
Caesar 44 B.C. / Columbus 1492 A.D. / Shakespeare 1616 A.D.
In fact, you can't even write a simple letter
without referring to Him: "March 7, 1980."
1980 what?
One thousand, nine hundred and eighty years
since the birth of a crucified Galilean Jew —
the most hated and loved person ever to walk on earth!
But why do men hate or love Jesus so?
Was He just another religious leader?
But other religious leaders led men to God:
"Israel, return to the Lord your God." (Hos 14:2)
Jesus led men to Himself
"Come to me . . . and I will give you rest." (Mt 11:28)
Do you know who Jesus is?
When you love someone, you want to learn all about him.
Isn't it time you began to learn more about Jesus?
Do you want to make it practical?
The Gospels are our main source of information about Him.
So make the following resolution *now:*
Every day read one chapter from the Gospels.
(Suggestion: Begin with John's.)
Read it slowly and prayerfully.
(That means no radio, stereo, or T.V.!)
Remember, the Gospels are four letters from God,
describing His great gift of love to men —
His only Son!

6 A house in Bethany, two miles outside Jerusalem. 12 years have passed since the last scene. It is near sunset. LAZARUS, a lad of 15, is at table with his two older sisters, MARTHA and MARY. There is a knock at the door. MARTHA answers.

Lk 2:41-45

MARTHA   Mary! Joseph! What brings you back?

MARY   Our Jesus — is he here?

MARTHA   Here? —
Why, he left yesterday morning in the caravan —

MARY   That's what we thought, too.
I assumed Joseph had him with the men in front.
Joseph took for granted he was behind with me.
Last night when we made camp,
we discovered he was gone — lost!

JOSEPH   (*heartsick*) This morning
the caravan continued on to Galilee,
but we retraced our steps.
I felt certain he would be with you,
since this is where we lodged for Passover.
Now our only hope is to find him in Jerusalem.

SISTER
MARY   No sense going on now. It's already late.
Have some supper and rest here tonight.
You can continue your search in the morning.

LAZARUS   Let's pray he's not been kidnapped
and carried off to Egypt as a slave.

SISTER
MARY   Or worse —
been run down by some Roman chariot.

MARTHA   Enough, you two! Let's have our supper.

On my bed at night, I dream of the one I love.
I looked for him but did not find him.
I will get up and go through the city,
in its streets and lanes
I will look for the one I love.

— *Song of Songs 3:1,2*

SEEING IS NOT BELIEVING

". . . they went back to Jerusalem looking for him." (Lk 2:45)
Some of the gospel stories are so familiar
that we recall how they end as soon as they start:
"Ah yes, they'll find him after three days."
We fail to realize that when it first happened,
those involved did not know how the story would end:
Mary wondered: "Is Jesus safe, kidnapped, or dead?"
The slogan "Seeing is believing" is false!
"Blessed are they who do *not* see and still believe." (Jn 20:29)
That's faith: believing in what we don't see. (Heb 11:1)
Abraham had it as he prepared to sacrifice Isaac.
Moses had it as he led the Israelites to the Promised Land.
Mary had it when she said "Yes" to Gabriel.
The centurion had it when he asked for his servant's cure.
"Without faith it is impossible to please God." (Heb 11:6)
That's what Jesus meant when He said:
"Unless you change and become like little children,
you will never enter the Kingdom of Heaven." (Mt 18:3)
"Like little children?"
Yes, for it takes child-like faith to believe in fairy tales.
Only children can see that bean-stalk reaching to heaven.
Only they can rejoice when the princess comes back to life.
When you give it some thought,
our Christian faith sounds very much like a fairy tale:
The prince left his castle in never-never land;
he disguised himself like the poorest in the realm.
He went about teaching young and old, rich and poor:
"If you want to get to my Father's Palace,
there is a narrow road, a winding road you must follow . . ."

19

Yes, Christianity does sound like a fairy-tale —
with this *one* difference:
It's absolutely true!
And you must be willing to die for that truth. (Mk 8:35)
"Whoever does not believe will be condemned." (Mk 16:16)
Strong words from One Who said He was gentle of heart!
But today, many (even some who say they're Christians)
put the Bible next to Grimm's and Aesop's fables.
"You don't expect us to believe in Adam and Eve,
and Original Sin, and all the rest of it, do you, Father?"
The question came from one of my students in religion class.
I began with a story from *Reader's Digest* (Dec. 76):
One evening, a Prof. Kenner was entertaining his friend,
engineer Buckminister Fuller, by the fireplace.
In popped three-year-old Lisa Kenner and asked:
"Bucky, why is the fire hot?"
Taking her on his lap, the engineer began:
"You remember when the tree was growing in the sunlight?"
On arms like upgroping branches,
his hands became clusters of leaves,
as he described their collecting the sunlight
and storing its energies in the stocky trunk.
"Then the men cut it down, and sawed it into logs.
And what you see now" — he pointed to the crackling hearth —
"is the sunlight, unwinding from the log."
When I had finished, I asked the student:
"Was the engineer telling that child a lie?"
"No, Father. That's what really happens."
"But he didn't mention photosynthesis or combustion or . . ."
"He would have been way over her head."
"I see. Well, in somewhat the same way,
you can say that the human race was just three years old,
when God revealed the first part of *Genesis*."

☆　　☆　　☆

"Unless you change and become like little children,
you will not enter the Kingdom of Heaven." (Mt 18:3)

7

The Temple in Jerusalem, the next morning. Seated around JESUS, a boy of 12, is a group of RABBIS, engaged in a debate.

Lk 2:46-52 / Mt 22:41-46

JESUS   When the Messiah comes,
whose descendant will he be?

RABBI   King David's, of course!
Why everyone knows that.

JESUS   Then why does David, inspired by God Himself,
refer to him as his Master:
    "The Lord God said to my *Master:*
    Sit here on my right
    until I crush your every enemy . . ."?
Would David have called the Messiah his *Master,*
if the Messiah were only his *offspring?*

RABBI   Hmmm. That problem never occured to us.

Enter MARY *and* JOSEPH.

MARY   Son, how could you do this to us?
Your father and I have been sick at heart,
searching for you everywhere!

JESUS   Why were you looking for me?
Didn't you realize that I would be right here
in my Father's house?

JOSEPH   Come, my son.
We have a long journey ahead of us to Nazareth.

☆   ☆   ☆

CHORUS *O Lord, I love the House where You Live,
the place where Your glory resides.*

— Psalm 26:8

21

"IN MY FATHER'S HOUSE"

From the time He disappears as a child in Nazareth
until He reappears as a man on the banks of the Jordan,
the curtain rises only once on Jesus:
He's a teenager, and — like most teens — in a jam!
"Son, how could you do this to us?" (Lk 2:48)
St. Luke preserves for us Jesus' recorded words:
"Didn't you know that I would be in my *Father's* House? (2:49)
Recall that Jesus was in the Temple — *God's* House!
So right from the start, He calls God His own Father.

COMPARE THESE STATISTICS:

In the Bible God is called *"Father"* 248 times:
only 14 times in the *entire* Old Testament,
166 times by Jesus (140 times as His personal Father!),
68 times in the rest of the New Testament.

☆   ☆   ☆

Lately, some theologians have been saying:
"Jesus didn't know who He was.
Only gradually did He come to realize He was God's Son."
Incredible! This opinion rings false for three reasons:

1. *It ignores Holy Scripture:*
   In the Temple — with Joseph standing there —
   Jesus clearly called God His own Father,
   to say nothing of the other 139 times!

2. *It ignores Church teaching:* (Calcedon 451 A.D.)
   It's the person who knows: "I know you."
   (No one says: "My *mind* knows you.")
   Jesus is only *one* person — a *divine* person.
   But someone ignorant of his own identity
   could not be divine.
   So Jesus had to know who He was.

22

3. *It ignores common sense:*
   A policeman asks a 5-year-old child who is lost:
   "Who are you?" — *"Johnny Smith."*
   "Who is your daddy?" — *"James Smith."*
   A liberal theologian asks the 12-year-old Jesus:
   "Who are you?" — *"Jesus from Nazareth."*
   "Who is your father?" — *"I don't know.*

   I've got to find out."
Speaking of His Father, Jesus once told the Pharisees:
"If I were to say I do not know Him,
I would be lying, like you.
But I do know Him . . ." (Jn 8:55)

☆　　☆　　☆

"He went back with them to Nazareth
and was OBEDIENT to them." (Lk 2:51)
Let's analyze that statement:
1. *Who was the one taking orders?*
   The very one, who in a few years
   would be *giving* orders to a killer-storm on the lake!
   His own disciples marveled: "Who can this be?
   Even the wind and the waves obey him!" (Mk 4:41)
   (To answer their question, read Psalm 107: 25-30.)
2. *Who were the ones giving orders?*
   Two simple parents from a poor village.
3. *Now then, can you imagine these words
   coming from someone who claims to be His follower?*
   "My old man is always on my back!
   I don't have to take that stuff from him any more!"

☆　　☆　　☆

Solution to the riddle in Mt 22:45:
Jesus is true God and true man:
As MAN, He's David's *offspring.* (Rm 1:3)
As GOD, He's David's *Master.* (Rm 1:4)

23

8 Some 18 years have passed since the last scene. We find ourselves at the Jordan River near Bethany. JOHN, the son of Zachary and Elizabeth, has grown to manhood. Dressed in a garment of camel's hair, he stands a stark figure by the river bank. CROWDS are gathered around him.

Lk 3:3-16 / Jn 1:19-34 / Mt 3:13-17

JOHN   Repent! The Lord is coming to save us!
        Prepare your hearts to welcome him!
        I warn you, put an end to your sinful ways
        or you shall all be lost!

RABBI   But we have Abraham for our father.
        We are the Lord's chosen people!

JOHN   I tell you, God can turn these dead river stones
        into living children of Abraham.
        So change your evil ways at once!

        A delegation of AUTHORITIES *from Jerusalem has been listening on the side. They approach* JOHN.

PRIEST Are you the Messiah we are expecting?

JOHN   No.

PRIEST Then you are Elijah?

JOHN   No, I'm not.

PRIEST Then you must be the prophet announced by Moses.

JOHN   I am not.

PRIEST Who are you then? Give us a clear answer
        to take back to our superiors in Jerusalem.

JOHN   I am only a voice in the desert, calling out
        the refrain from Isaiah the prophet:

24

> "Prepare the way for the Lord.
> Straighten out the path before Him.
> Tear down those mountains of your vices,
> and fill those empty valleys with goodness."

PRIEST   If you are not the prophet, Elijah, or the Messiah,
           by what right are you baptizing?

JOHN   I use water to baptize.
           But the one coming after me
           will baptize you with the Holy Spirit.
           He is much, much greater than I.
           I am not fit to stoop down and undo his sandals.
           The DELEGATION *exits.* JOHN *wades into the water
           and begins baptizing the waiting crowds. Enter*
           JESUS, *now a man of 30. He approaches* JOHN.

JESUS   I have come to be baptized.

JOHN   But *you* should be the one to baptize *me*.

JESUS   This must be done to fulfill my Father's plan.

           JESUS *removes his robe and enters the river.
           Reluctantly* JOHN *takes him and immerses him
           beneath the surface. As* JESUS *comes up, a cloud
           appears over him, and a dove comes down on him.*

VOICE   (*like a thunder-clap from the cloud*)

           This is My only Son!
           In him is My delight!

           JESUS *leaves the water, dons his robe and exits.*

JOHN   There goes the Lamb of God.
           He will rid the world of all its sin.

ANDREW   (*approaching* JOHN) Rabbi, who was that?

JOHN   I wasn't sure he was the one,
           but now I am.
           When God sent me to baptize, He told me:
           "The one on whom you see the Spirit come to rest
           like a dove from heaven,

will be the one to baptize in the Holy Spirit."
Now I am certain that he is the Son of God!

CHORUS   *Thus says the Lord:*
          "This is my servant, my chosen one,
          in whom my soul takes great delight.
          I have poured my spirit upon him,
          and he will bring justice to all the nations."

                                        —*Isaiah 42:1*

THE BIBLE: GOD'S LOVE LETTER TO US

The voice from the cloud spoke twice over Jesus:
at His baptism and again when He was transfigured.
Both times the message was the same:
"This is my Son — the One I love. Listen to Him." (Mt 17:5)
Whenever the prophets had spoken in the past,
they urged the people: "Hear the word of the Lord."
Now God Himself pleads with us to listen to His WORD,
Who became one of us to teach us about the Father. (Jn 1:18)
That's what is meant in the letter to the Hebrews:
"Formerly God spoke to our ancestors through the *prophets,*
but now He has spoken to us through His *Son."* (Heb 1:1)
The Bible is a collection of the times God spoke to us:
the Old Testament repeats: "He is coming! He is coming!"
the New Testament says: "Rejoice! Our Savior is here!"
Our Protestant brothers have such a love for the Bible
that they say God speaks to us *only* through the Scriptures.
We Catholics hold that God *also* speaks to us
through the living voice of His teaching Church (*Magisterium*).
We can show this from Holy Scripture itself:
Mt 28:20 Jesus did not command His disciples to write
   or to put a copy of the Bible in everyone's hands.
   Rather, "*Teach* all men to observe everything I told you."
Lk 10:16 "Whoever *hears* you, hears me."
Rm 10:17 "Faith comes through *hearing* the good news,
   and hearing comes through *preaching* Christ."
1 Co 15:1,2 St. Paul reminds his converts at Corinth
   that they are being *saved* if they continue to *believe*
   the gospel "which I *preached* to you."

Were those Corinthians true Christians? Of Course!
Yet they never had a copy of the New Testament!
Ac 8:30-35 The eunuch does not understand the passage
of Isaiah he is reading until Philip explains it to him.
What does this say about interpreting the Bible privately?
2 Pt 3:16 Peter rules out private interpretation:
"In Paul's letters some things are hard to understand,
which ignorant and unstable people misinterpret —
as they do the rest of Scripture —
to their own destruction."
Accordingly, Scripture needs an official interpreter.
That official voice is the Church's teaching authority.
The Voice of God is like a coin with two sides:
Holy Scripture AND the *teaching Church.*
St. Paul says this very thing in 2 Th 2:15:
"And so, my brothers, continue to stand firm
and hold on to the teachings which you learned from us,
whether it was by *word of mouth* or in *writing."*
"word of mouth" = Paul's preaching to them in person;
"writing" = the first letter to the Thessalonians.
With this important distinction made, it's tragic but true,
that for most Catholics the Bible is still a closed book.
"Ignorance of Scripture is ignorance of Christ." (St. Jerome)
Back in the fifth scene it was suggested
that you become more familiar with Jesus
by reading one chapter of the Gospels every day.
Have you done that — even once since then?
"I've been too busy!"
Too busy? But you always find time
for the things that you consider important in life.
You may be up to your ears in work,
but when that special friend calls you on the phone,
you drop everything else — even for hours — just to talk.
So if you don't find time for God,
frankly, it's because He doesn't rate with you!
How much time do you spend each day watching T.V.?
Or gossiping on the phone?
Or reading the newspaper?
Do you spend as much time reading Scripture

as you do — let's say — the comic section?
Who is more important: Dick Tracy or Jesus?
Could you apply the following to the daily paper?
"All Scripture is inspired by God and is useful
for teaching the truth,
for rejecting error,
for correcting faults,
for moulding character . . ." (2 Tm 3:16)

9 The desert to the north of Jerico, 40 days later, JESUS, lost in prayer, lies prostrate on the ground. A shadow falls across the sand.

Mt 4:1-11

SATAN   (*aside*) It's been forty days
since he last touched food.
What superhuman will power!
And a mere carpenter —
Or could he be something more?
Perhaps a heavenly spirit in disguise. —
That voice at the Jordan did say, "my son."
Could he be . . .? (*He approaches* JESUS.)
Are you the son of God? —
Then change these stones to loaves of bread.

JESUS   (*rising slowly to his feet*) It is written:
"Not on bread alone is man to live,
but on every word that is uttered
by the mouth of God."

In an instant, SATAN *transports* JESUS *to Jerusalem,
to the highest tower of the Temple.*

SATAN   Do you see that crowd below?
They are praying for the coming of their Messiah.
Prove to them that you are the Son of God
by hurling yourself down.
For it is written:
"He has put His angels in charge of you.
With their very hands they will rescue you,
to keep you from striking your foot
against a single stone."

JESUS	It also says in scripture: "You are not to tempt the Lord your God."
	SATAN *transfers* JESUS *to a lofty mountain peak.*
SATAN	Look — there in the distance — Tyre — Sidon — Alexandria — Athens — Rome! What grandeur! What magnificence! And they all belong to *me!* But I am willing to give them to *you,* provided you fall down and worship me!
JESUS	Get away from me, Satan! For it is written: "The Lord your God you are to worship. Him alone you shall adore!"
	Exit SATAN. *Enter* ANGELS *to comfort* JESUS.

☆ ☆ ☆

CHORUS	*The woman answered the Serpent:* *"We may eat the fruit of any tree* *except for the tree in the middle of the garden.* *God told us not even to touch it.* *If we do, we shall die."* *The Serpent replied: "No, you shall not die.* *For God knows that when you eat it,* *you shall be like Him, perceiving good and evil."*
	— Genesis 3:1-4

SPIRITS: GOOD AND EVIL

Does Satan have horns and a tail, and use a pitchfork?
Do angels have wings and play the harp?
If not, why do we imagine them that way?
Or could it be that they don't exist at all?
To answer these questions, try solving this problem:
Describe a sunset to a person who was born blind.
"It's a beautiful orange ball with scarlet hues above . . ."
"Orange? Scarlet? What are you talking about?"
"Well — it's peaceful like the soft music of a violin,
and ah — it's smooth like velvet . . ."

Would our blind friend be justified in concluding:
"Forget it! Sunsets don't exist!
I've never experienced one."?
Yet that's precisely what many people do
when it comes to things of the spirit.
They conclude that it's a make-believe world.
They fail to realize that man is a creature of two worlds:
material and spiritual.
The following illustration may clarify this point:

SCALE OF EXISTENCE

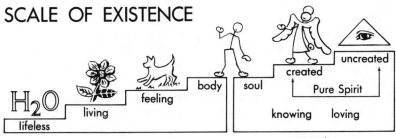

Through our *body* we see, hear, and feel like the animals.
Through our *soul* we can think and love.
Does an animal know who its grandparents were?
Can an animal go on a hunger strike?
Of course not. It operates on instinct.
It has no choice. It *must* eat when it feels hungry.
But man can choose to starve, if he wishes.
The power to *think* and to *choose* proves
that we are citizens of another world — a *spiritual* world!
But in that world, we are like the blind man and the sunset.
We must have someone describe it for us:
"No one has ever seen God.
The only Son, Who was always near the Father,
came to tell us all about Him." (Jn 1:18)
Would He have misled us in a matter so important?
Impossible!
The spiritual formed part and parcel of Jesus' message:
"My kingdom is not of this world." (Jn 18:36)

31

ANGELS announced His coming and sang at His birth.
They comforted Him after He was tempted by Satan.
They appeared at the empty tomb and at His ascension.
They will accompany Him when He returns in glory.
On other occasions Jesus also spoke of FALLEN ANGELS:
He saw Satan fall like lightning from heaven. (Lk 10:18)
(This fall is described by St. John in Rv 12:7-9.
All creatures, including angels, were created
to reflect God's goodness.
The angels, endowed with free will, could choose.
Some chose to rebel and so were cast from God's presence.)
Hell was created for the devil and his angels. (Mt 25:41)
Jesus called Satan "the prince of this world" (Jn 14:30)
and the "father of lies." (Jn 8:44)
Peter was later to reinforce Jesus' teaching:
"Be alert and stay awake!
For your enemy the devil prowls about like a roaring lion,
in search of someone to devour." (1 Pt 5:8)
Yes, we are citizens of a material and a spiritual world.
Which is the more important?
"The world we see will have an end.
The world of the spirit will last forever." (2 Co 4:18)
Jesus said the same thing in Mk 8:36:
"What have you gained by mastering the whole world,
if you should then lose your immortal soul?"
Helen Keller, who was both blind and deaf,
echoed the same thought in this simple poem:
"They took away what should have been my eyes
(But I remembered Milton's *Paradise*).
They took away what should have been my ears
(Beethoven came and wiped away my tears).
They took away what should have been my tongue
(But I had talked with God when I was young).
He would not let them take away my soul —
Possessing that, I still possess the whole."

10

A week later. Capernaum, a fishing town on the northwest shore of the Sea of Galilee. It is early morning. In a boat, two brothers, JAMES and JOHN, are helping their father ZEBEDEE mend his fishing nets.

Jn 1:35-42 / Mt 4:17-25; 13:45-50 / Lk 5:1-4

JAMES   So you and Andrew just started to follow him?

JOHN   Not exactly. He came walking along
while we were standing with the Baptist.
John was the one who pointed him out to us:
"There goes the Lamb of God."
That's when we followed behind.
After a short distance, he turned and asked,
"What are you looking for?"
I said, "Rabbi, where are you staying?"
"Come and see," he told us.
We went and stayed with him the rest of the day.
James, if you had only been there!
Andrew was so excited
that the next day he found his brother Simon . . .
James, look! — There he is!

JAMES   You mean, the Rabbi Jesus? (*Enter* JESUS)

JOHN   Yes, and he's coming this way!

JESUS   (*looking intently at the* BROTHERS)
Come with me.
I will make you fish for men's souls.
The TWO *leave the boat and follow. They continue
along the shore until they encounter a* CROWD
around SIMON'S *boat.*

34

PASSERBY	(*from a distance*) Simon, any fish for sale?
PETER	Not a single one! The night was a total waste!
JESUS	(*approaching*) Someday, Simon, I will have you fishing for men. (*He climbs aboard then turns and continues in a loud voice.*) Come, and hear the good news! (*A* CROWD *gathers and moves in.*) Turn away from your sins, for the Kingdom of God is here! That kingdom is like a rare and precious pearl. A jeweler searches for it far and wide, and when he finds it, he goes off to sell everything he has so that he can buy that one rare pearl. The Kingdom of God is also like a fishing net that's cast out into the sea. It catches all kinds of fish. When it is full, the fishermen haul it in and sit on the shore to separate the catch: the good fish are put into baskets, the useless ones are thrown away. That is how it will be at the end of the world: the angels will go out and separate sinners from saints. The sinners will be cast into the fires of hell, where they will weep and suffer forever.

☆ ☆ ☆

CHORUS	*The Lord God said to me:* *"Before I formed you in the womb, I called you* *to be a prophet to the nations."* *"Ah, Lord God," I answered,* *"I don't know how to speak. I am so young."* *But the Lord said to me:* *"Do not tell me you are too young,* *for you shall go to the people I send you to* *and tell them whatever I command you."* — *Jeremiah 1:4-7*

A CALL TO SACRIFICE

By the time Alexander was 30,
he had carved an empire from Greece to India.
And Augustus at 30 was master of the civilized world.
By the time Jesus was 30,
He had worn calluses on His hands in a carpenter shop.
In less than three years, He would be gone.
In the interval, His main task was to choose and train
a group of men to be His followers.
There were only twelve in that inner circle:
common laborers, simple fishermen, a tax collector —
on the whole, a group not especially noted for brilliance.
How frequently Jesus had to correct them:
Mt 16:9 "Are you still without any understanding?"
Mt 8:26 "Why were you afraid? What little faith you have!"
Mk 10:42 "Pagan leaders rule with an iron hand,
            but it should not be that way with you."
Jn 14:9 "Philip, have I been with you all this time,
            and you still don't know me?"
For three years they were with Him night and day:
they ate and drank with Him,
they saw Him sink to sleep from exhaustion,
they heard Him hush the storm to silence,
and helped Him distribute the bread to the hungry crowd;
they listened intently as He spoke to them of God.
On their simple ears fell the message
that kings and prophets had wanted to hear. (Lk 10:24)
Jesus spoke to the crowds only in obscure parables,
but to His disciples He explained everything in private.
"You have been chosen to learn the inner secrets
of the Kingdom of God . . ." (Mt 13:11)
Jesus' public life was little more than a training school
for His twelve Apostles. They were to be His generals,
sent forth to conquer the world in His name:
"You are to be my witnesses
in Jerusalem, in all of Judea and Samaria,
and even to the ends of the earth." (Ac 1:8)
Yet the message was not to disappear with them.

Others were to replace them when they had died.
Before leaving them, Jesus had prayed:
"Father, I pray not only for my disciples,
but also for those who will come to believe in me
because of their message." (Jn 17:20)
After the Lord's ascension, Peter addressed the Apostles:
"We must choose someone to replace Judas,
to act as witness to the Lord's resurrection." (Ac 1:22-25)
Now then, what do you think of the following words?
"Thousands of martyrs have heroically laid down their lives.
Let us hold high their banner and march ahead
along the path crimson with their blood."
Does it sound familiar? St. Ignatius perhaps? Or a pope?
You're wrong. It's a quote from
Chairman Mao Tse-Tung, the former leader of Red China.
He was prodding the youth of China in 1945 to face death
in order to spread the godlessness of Communism.
How tragic! God's enemies are willing to sacrifice all
for a reward that will not last,
and we are so reluctant to make a small sacrifice
for a reward that will last forever. (1 Co 9:25)
The Lord may be inviting you to give yourself to Him
as He invited Mary to become His Mother,
or James and John to become His followers.
We have His assurance that there is no happier life:
"Anyone who has left home or brothers or sisters
or father or mother or children or property for my sake,
will receive *a hundred times more* in this world
and *eternal life* in the next." (Mt 19:29)

11

Three days later. Cana, near Nazareth. A wedding celebration has been in progress for two days. GUESTS overflow into the patio, as sounds of singing and laughter fill the air. MARY, the mother of JESUS, crosses to the WAITERS.

Jn 2:1-11

MARY

(*handing a pitcher to a* WAITER)
I would like some wine.
My son has just arrived with his friends.

WAITER

Sorry. We just ran out.

MARY

(*after a moment's thought*) Come with me.
(*The* WAITERS *cross with her to* JESUS.)
They are out of wine.

JESUS

(*softly*) Why do you bring that up to me?
My hour, woman, has not yet come.

MARY

(*turning to the* WAITERS)
Do whatever he tells you.

JESUS *crosses to the vestibule with the* WAITERS.
There are six stone water jars near the entrance.

JESUS

Fill these jars with water.
(*Time passes as the* WAITERS *fill them to the brim.*
Then JESUS *raises his eyes to heaven.*)
Now take a sample of this to the best man.

WAITER *dips a goblet, then crosses to the*
BEST MAN.

WAITER

Sir, be good enough to sample this.

BEST MAN

(*savoring the wine*) Superb!
And I was told that you were running short!

(*crosses to the* GROOM)

Josiah, what a delightful prank!
Everyone else serves the good wine first.
Then, when the guests have been drinking a while,
out comes the common wine!
But you have kept the best wine for last!

NATHANIEL   (*aside to* JOHN) Incredible!
They poured water into those jugs.
John, who do you suppose this rabbi is?

JOHN   I don't know, Nathaniel. I just don't know.

CHORUS   *Wisdom built a house for herself.*
She slaughtered the beasts, mixed her wine,
and prepared the table.
"Come, dine with me
and drink the wine that I have poured."
                   — *Proverbs 9:1-5*

IS GOD GLOOMY?

"You have saved the best wine until now." (Jn 2:10)
Too often we have a dismal image of God.
A teenager once defined God as
"the One who's always sneaking up on you
to make sure you're not having any fun."
That youngster had it just backwards.
All real happiness in life comes from God.
Take eating, for example — it's something we *have* to do.
But instead of a chore, God made it a pleasure.
Most foods contain carbon. So does gasoline.
So if God had designed our stomachs somewhat differently,
instead of having lunch at McDonald's,
we might be having it at Exxon's!
Yes, God wants us to be happy.
As the old catechism said: "God made me
to know Him, to love Him, and to serve Him in this world,
and *to be happy* with Him forever in the next."
Now then, for some questions:
"Is it a sin to go to parties?"

Would Jesus have gone to the wedding feast of Cana?
"Is it a sin to drink?"
Would Jesus have changed water into wine?
"Is it a sin to get drunk?"
Yes! "Don't you know that drunkards will not inherit
the Kingdom of God?" (1 Co 6:10)
Alcohol is a gift from God.
But like all gifts, it must be used properly.
To abuse it is an insult both to God and to yourself.
You insult *God* by cheapening one of His blessings.
You insult *yourself* by telling the world you're immature.
Alcoholism is an epidemic!
There are an estimated 10 million alcoholics in America.
Intoxication has caused
    more lost jobs,
    more traffic deaths,
    more battered wives,
    more abused children,
    more broken homes than any other single factor!
One is almost tempted to agree with the fundamentalists,
who say that drinking was invented by Satan.
And yet — Jesus did make over 100 gallons of wine!
Besides, many people tell lies.
Should we then say that speech is an invention of Satan?
Of course not! We correct the abuse, but keep the gift.
Moderate drinking is a gift from God. (Ps 104:15)
That's something to remember
the next time someone asks you at a party:
"Let's get bombed tonight!"
Moderate drinking is for the mature.
Getting drunk is for misfits.
Moderate drinking can give real pleasure.
Getting drunk gives nothing but misery here,
and eternal punishment in hell!

☆   ☆   ☆

Mary said to Jesus, "They have no wine." (Jn 2:3)
Sometimes our non-Catholic friends criticize us:
"By praying to Mary you Catholics make a goddess out of her.
You should pray only to God."

40

At Mass and the Liturgy of the Hours
— even on feasts of the saints —
the Church directs her prayers to God alone.
At other times, however, she encourages us to pray
directly to the saints to intercede for us with God.
(St. Paul asked that of mere converts! Eph 6:19, Col 4:3)
Besides, we have the actual example of Mary
persuading Jesus to break His Father's time-schedule
and begin His public life early: "They are out of wine."
If she had not intervened, there would have been no miracle!
In Mary's beautiful prayer — the rosary —
we approach to tell her that we are running out
of the rich wine of her Son's saving grace:
"Holy Mary, Mother of God, pray for us sinners . . ."

12

Jerusalem, two weeks later. The Temple court of the Gentiles. The scene is more like a stockyard: cattle, sheep, and cages of doves stacked high. The air reeks with the stench of dung. MERCHANTS vie for trade as MONEYCHANGERS convert Roman coins to Temple currency.

Jn 2:13-22

MERCHANT   Passover lambs! Tender lambs for the feast day!

JESUS   (*entering suddenly*) Is it not written:
"My house is to be a house of prayer?"
But you have made it a den of thieves!

He takes up some rope and knots it into a whip. He begins lashing to right and left. He overturns the tables of the MONEYCHANGERS.

MERCHANTS   (*together*) What is this?
               Guards, stop him!
               He's after blood! Help!

JESUS   (*to the* DOVE SELLERS) Get these out of here!
Stop turning my Father's House into a market
    place!

Some minutes of general confusion follow, as MERCHANTS *and animals go scampering. Enter* PRIESTS *and* GUARDS. *They approach* JESUS.

PRIEST   By what right have you done this?
Show us a sign from God to justify your actions!

JESUS   (*gesturing with his hands on his chest*)
Destroy this Temple,
and in three days I will raise it up!

PRIEST	They've been building this Temple for 46 years, and you're going to raise it up in three days! You must be insane!

☆ ☆ ☆

CHORUS	*The Lord you await will suddenly come to His Temple.*
	And who can withstand the day of his coming?
	He will purify the priests like silver and gold.
	Then they will make a worthy offering to the Lord.

—Malachi 3:1-3

KEEP THE LORD'S DAY HOLY

Let's say that you receive a letter from the White House.
Your heart skips a beat as you open it:
"The President cordially invites you
to join him for dinner next Sunday."
What would your reaction be?
"Wow! What an honor! I'll be the envy of the class."
Suppose your response had been one of the following?
"Do I have to go?"
"I'll be bored."
"But I like to sleep late on Sundays."
"Sorry! I made plans to go to the football game."
Would such a response show any respect for the President?
Yet that's precisely how some people treat God.
Through His Church, He invites us to a banquet every week.
At Mass God reenacts for us the sacrifice of Calvary
in the form of a banquet:
"Eat, this is my body . . . Drink, this is my blood . . ."
But how do we respond to the Lord's invitation?
"Do I have to go?"
Do you *have* to see your date next Saturday night?
"I'm too busy."
Too busy to give God *one* hour out of 168?
"But I'm bored at Mass. I get nothing out of it."
Are you going to Church to be entertained?
Or to tell God how much you need Him and love Him?
"But God knows I love Him. He understands."

43

Understands your indifference? Really?
Read what He has to say in Malachi 1:6-14:
His chosen people had been offering Him leftovers:
lambs with diseased wool or with broken legs:
"A curse on the one who offers me a sick animal
when he still has a healthy lamb in his flock.
If you gave an animal like that to your governor,
would he accept it? Would you get any favors from him?"
Then God goes on to predict — centuries in advance —
the end of the Jewish sacrifices in the Temple
and the world-wide offering of the sacrifice of the Mass:
"When will someone shut the doors of the Temple
to keep you from lighting worthless fires on my altar?
I am not pleased with you, says the Lord of Hosts,
and I will no longer accept a sacrifice from you.
For all over the world I am honored among the gentiles,
and everywhere they offer me a pure sacrifice." (vv. 10 & 11)
How thrilled you should be that, as a Catholic,
you help to make that prophecy come true every week.
To offer some pretext for missing Mass is a cop-out.
Besides, if you don't worship God in Church on Sunday,
just how do you keep the Lord's day holy?
How do you differ from someone who's an atheist?
He sleeps in on Sunday — so do you.
He shops on Sunday — so do you.
Is that honoring the Lord on His day —
business as usual?
Jesus drove the merchants from His Father's House —
and they were selling animals required for the sacrifice!
What would He do in a local shopping mall on Sunday?
God deserves the best, not second-best.
"Be holy, for I the Lord your God am holy." (Lv 29:2)
Remember to keep holy the Sabbath Day.

44

13

Jerusalem. It is late at night in a private home, one week later. JESUS is seated with a few of his DISCIPLES. There is a knock; JOHN answers. Enter NICODEMUS, a Pharisee.

Jn 3:1-16

NICODEMUS   (*seating himself next to* JESUS)
Rabbi, I would like some advice.
I am convinced
that you have come from God to teach us.
For no one could do the miraculous things you do
unless God were with him.

JESUS   What is it that you want to know?

NICODEMUS   I was puzzled
by what you told the people yesterday.
I mean, the matter about rebirth.

JESUS   It's true. Whoever is not born from above
will never see the Kingdom of God.

NICODEMUS   But how can that be?
Can a grown man return to his mother's womb
and be born again?

JESUS   You cannot get into God's Kingdom,
unless you are born of water and the Spirit.
You came into this world through a physical birth.
To enter God's world, you need a spiritual birth.
You look surprised because I said:
You have to be born from above.
Take the wind, for example; it is mysterious.
You can hear it blowing,

	though you don't know where it comes from, or where it's going. It blows wherever it pleases. Spiritual birth is something like that.
NICODEMUS	It doesn't seem possible.
JESUS	How can you teach others, if you don't understand these things yourself? I am telling you what I actually know. I am an eye-witness, yet you will not take my word. If you refuse to believe me concerning the things of this world, how will you believe me when I describe those of heaven to you?
NICODEMUS	You know — what goes on — in heaven?
JESUS	As the Son of Man, I came down from heaven. And I am the only one who has a right to return to heaven. But first I must be lifted up on earth. You recall how Moses in the desert lifted up the bronze serpent on the stake to save from death all who looked on it. That is how I must be lifted up, so that everyone who believes in me will live forever. Yes, the Father loved the world so much, that He sent His only Son to save it.

☆   ☆   ☆

CHORUS	*Thus says the Lord of Hosts:* *"I will pour clean water over you,* *and I will purify you of all your filth.* *I will give you a new heart and a new spirit.* *I shall replace your heart of stone* *with a heart of flesh.*

— Ezekiel 36:25-27

BORN INTO GOD'S FAMILY

May 7, 1959 was a balmy day in San Francisco.
Shirley O'Neill and Al Kogler were cooling off in the bay
when, without warning, a shark snapped off Al's left arm.
Shirley brought him in — a stream of blood trailing behind.
Safe at last on shore, she scooped up some sea water
and poured it over Al's forehead:
"I baptize thee in the name of the Father
and of the Son and of the Holy Spirit. —
Is that all right?" she whispered.
"O.K.," he gasped.
(On their dates they had often discussed religion.
Al had none. He was 18 but had never been baptized.)
Just before he fell unconscious, Albert whispered:
"I love God, and I love my mother and I love my father.
O God, help me."
Two hours later, he was dead — and born into eternal life.

☆　　☆　　☆

St. Paul describes baptism in the same way —
a strange mixture of death and life:
"In baptism you were buried with Christ,
in baptism you were also raised with Christ." (Col 2:12)
Let us examine the Church's teaching on baptism.
It goes back to that tragic day when Adam rejected God:
"One man brought sin into the world,
and with sin came death.
And so all men must die,
because in Adam all have sinned." (Rm 5:12)
In this verse, St. Paul is describing original sin.
He refers to what God revealed in Genesis, chapter 3.
As a Catholic, you must believe:
1. The human race descended from *one* set of parents.
2. God blessed our first parents with His friendship (*grace*).
3. To prove their friendship, they had to undergo a *test*.
4. They failed the test; they deliberately *rejected* God.
5. Their sin of rebellion was *passed on* to all of us.
On the surface, this teaching seems unjust:
Why should we have to suffer for what our forebears did?

But compare the situation to that of some children
who are born in dire poverty:
their grandfather had gambled and lost the family fortune!
Many years ago Chesterton observed:
Certain new theologians dispute original sin, which is
the only part of Christianity which can really be proven!
Confronted with evil and suffering in the world,
we must either deny the existence of God, as atheists do,
or admit a breach between God and man, as Christians do.
Simply stated: To prove that original sin is a reality,
just consult the crime cases in today's newspaper
or pay a visit to the insane asylum.
A thinking person must conclude:
Something is *radically* wrong in human nature.
That radical evil we call original sin.
It was to restore man to His friendship
— to undo the evil that Adam had done —
that God sent His only Son to be our Savior.
Now read Romans, chapters 5 and 6, where St. Paul describes
how God adopts us into His family.
ROMANS 5:12-6:23

WHO?	Adam	Christ
DID WHAT?	disobeyed God	obeyed God
WHERE?	tree of Eden	tree of the Cross
RESULT?	sin	grace
HOW TRANSMITTED?	physical birth	spiritual birth (*baptism*)
EFFECT?	death	life

In chapter 6, St. Paul compares baptism to a burial:
As one is immersed in the waters of baptism,
he leaves his sins buried there ("he dies to sin").
As he comes up out of the water, he rises to a new life —
a sharing in God's own life through the Holy Spirit:
"Now that you are His children,
God has sent the Spirit of His Son into our hearts,
giving us the right to call Him "Abba! Father!" (Ga 4:6)
That's what Jesus meant when He told Nicodemus:
"Unless you are born of water and the Spirit,
you cannot enter the Kingdom of God." (Jn 3:5)

<table>
<tr><td>

14

</td><td>

Two weeks have passed since the last scene. It is high noon as JESUS and his DISCIPLES near the outskirts of Sychar, a town in central Samaria.

</td></tr>
</table>

Jn 4:1-42

JESUS   Go on into the town for provisions,
while I rest here by the well.

As the DISCIPLES *leave,* JESUS *sits at the well and wipes the sweat from his brow. Enter a* WOMAN *with a large water jug on her head. Ignoring* JESUS, *she ties a rope to the jug and lowers it into the well. She retrieves it with great exertion.*

JESUS   Give me a drink.

WOMAN   (*startled*) How *dare* you! You're a Jew! —
Yet you ask *me,* a Samaritan, for a drink?!

JESUS   If you only knew about God's gift,
and who I am,
you would have asked *me* for a drink
of refreshing water.

WOMAN   Nonsense! This well is quite deep, sir,
and you haven't a thing to draw water with.
Just how do you plan to get that refreshing water?
Surely you don't pretend to be greater
than our ancestor Jacob, do you?
He gave us this well!

JESUS   This water will only make you thirsty again.
But the water I give
will quench your thirst forever.
It will become a living fountain inside of you,
giving life everlasting.

49

WOMAN	Please, sir, give me some of that water, so that I won't get thirsty again and have to return here day after day.
JESUS	Go and get your husband for me.
WOMAN	I have no husband.
JESUS	That's a fact — you *don't* have a husband. For you have had five of them already. So the man you're living with now is not really your husband.
WOMAN	Sir, I can tell you're a man of God. Perhaps you can solve this problem for me then: Where should we worship God: on Mount Gerizim, where we Samaritans do, or in Jerusalem, where you Jews have your Temple?
JESUS	You do not have authentic worship, but we do; for salvation comes from the Jews. Still, the time is coming, woman, when you will worship the Father neither on this mountain nor in Jerusalem. True worshipers must worship the Father in spirit and truth. Since God is spirit, He wants His worship to be deeply spiritual.
WOMAN	We Samaritans believe in the Messiah, too. When he comes, he will teach us everything.
JESUS	I am the Messiah!

Suddenly, enter the DISCIPLES.

ANDREW	(*to* JOHN) Why is he talking to that woman? What do you suppose she wants?

Exit WOMAN, *forgetting her water jug.*

PETER	Master, we brought you some food.
JESUS	I have food to eat that you know nothing about.
PETER	(*aside to* JOHN) Could someone have brought him food while we were gone?

50

JESUS	My nourishment comes from doing my Father's will and completing His work here on earth.

JESUS   My nourishment comes from doing my Father's will
and completing His work here on earth.
Anyone will tell you
that harvest time is still four months away.
But I tell you, look up and see the fields
just ripe with souls to be harvested.
(Enter off in the distance WOMAN *with*
    VILLAGERS.)*

The harvest was planted by others before you —
the prophets; but I am sending you out
to bring in the fruits of their labors.
That way, the ones who did the planting,
as well as those who do the harvesting,
will rejoice together in heaven.

WOMAN   *(to the* VILLAGERS) Here he is —
the prophet who told me everything I ever did!

TOWN   Sir, we would be honored to have you stay
LEADER   in our village for a few days as our guest.
Our friend here has made some fantastic claims.
But we would like to find out for ourselves
whether or not you really are
the Savior of the world!

☆   ☆   ☆

CHORUS   *There are two sins that my people have committed:*
They have rejected Me,
the fountain of living water;
and they have dug cisterns for themselves —
leaky cisterns — that can hold no water.
                       — Jeremiah 2:13

GRACE: A FLOWING RIVER OF LIFE

St. Paul uses the word "grace" over 80 times in his letters.
But exactly what is it?
Bishop Fulton Sheen once used a simple story to explain it:
Suppose that one evening a stray dog follows you home.
You take him in, wash him, and feed him.
Weeks pass. You train him and become quite attached.

But no matter how attached you become,
you stand radically apart; for he cannot communicate.
One day a scientist invents a special "human-life" serum
and shoots 20 cc's of this wonder liquid into your pet.
Your dog now takes on human traits.
While still keeping the outward appearance of a dog,
he can converse with you in human terms. For example,
he can tell you what a rough day he had at the kennels.
Your dog now shares *human life* with you.
You can set a place for him at your dinner table,
and even adopt him into your family, if you wish.
This example sheds some light on what grace does.
Simply stated, grace is our sharing in God's life!
It's the "divine-life" serum, so to speak,
that God poured into our souls at baptism.
On that day He lifted us up from the merely human:
He would later invite us to converse with Him in prayer
and sit at His supper table at Holy Mass.
In a word, He adopted us into His own family!
Jesus expressed a similar idea
when He used the example of a growing vine:
"I am the vine, you are the branches.
If you remain joined to me, you will bear much fruit;
for without me, you can do nothing." (Jn 15:5)
Like tender branches, we were grafted onto Jesus at baptism.
As long as we remain attached to Him (the trunk),
the "sap" of divine grace continues to flow from Him to us.
Only deliberate sin can cut us off from Him:
"Whoever separates himself from me
is thrown away like a branch and dries up.
Such branches are collected and burned in a bonfire." (v. 6)
(To go back to our example of the "humanized" dog:
It would be just as if he had returned to the pack
and began to snap at the children in the neighborhood.
The only alternative open is to call the dog pound
and have him taken away to be gassed.)
Grace is something quite intangible.
Jesus Himself never used the word.
Instead, He preferred the terms "water" and "life".

Jn 4:14 "The water that I give
will become a fountain inside of him,
giving *life* everlasting."

Jn 7:37 "Anyone who is thirsty should come to me and drink.
For as the scripture says,
'Rivers of living water will flow
from the hearts of those who believe in me.' "

In these passages, Jesus is claiming divinity,
for in the O.T. only *God* could quench spiritual thirst:

Ps 42 "As a deer longs for running streams,
so do I long for You, my God.
My soul thirsts for God, the God of *life*."

Ps 63 "My God, I long for You.
Just like waterless land that is parched dry,
that's how my soul is thirsting for You."

15

Several months have passed. JESUS is seated on the slope of a hill in Galilee, looking down on a vast CROWD, seated around him as if in an amphitheater. They listen intently as he preaches what follows.

Mt 5:1-18; 38-48 / 6:24-34 / 7:12

JESUS　　How happy are the poor and lowly —
　　　　　the Kingdom of God is theirs!
　　　　Happy are those who weep —
　　　　　their tears will be wiped away!
　　　　Happy are those who long for justice —
　　　　　their hunger shall be satisfied!
　　　　Happy are the merciful —
　　　　　mercy shall be theirs!
　　　　Happy are the pure in heart —
　　　　　for they shall see God!
　　　　Happy the peacemakers —
　　　　　they shall be called children of God!
　　　　Happy are those oppressed unjustly —
　　　　　for theirs is the Kingdom of Heaven!

☆　　☆　　☆

I have not come to set aside what the prophets foretold.
　　but rather, to bring it to fulfillment.
Remember, before heaven and earth pass away,
　　every last detail of scripture must all come true.
The Law says: "An eye for an eye and a tooth for a tooth."
　　But I say to you: Never seek revenge at all.
If someone slaps you on the right cheek,
　　offer him your left cheek, too.
If someone tries to steal your coat,
　　let him take your shirt as well.
If someone forces you to carry his pack one mile,

go with him an extra mile besides.
The Law says: "Love your friends and hate your enemies."
    But I say: Love your enemies and bless your oppressors.
You must become like your Father in heaven:
    He makes His sun come up on good and bad alike,
    and sends His rain on both the sinner and the saint.
If you love only those who love you,
    what reward can you expect? Even sinners do that!
And if you say "hello" only to your friends,
    what is so extraordinary? The pagans do as much!
But *you* must be perfect —
    just as your heavenly Father is perfect!
All of Holy Scripture can be summed up in this one command:
    Treat others as you want them to treat you.

☆　　☆　　☆

No one can serve two masters:
    in time you will betray the trust of one of them.
You must choose, then, bewteen God and worldly concerns.
    That's why I tell you:
Do not worry about what you shall eat and drink,
    or about the clothes you are to wear.
Isn't your soul more precious than food,
    and your body, more important than clothing?
Consider the birds in the sky:
    they do not plant and harvest and store away in barns,
    yet your heavenly Father gives them food.
Aren't you much more valuable than all the birds together?
And as for your clothing, why do you worry?
    Consider the flowers in the meadow:
they don't weave or sew garments for themselves.
    Yet, I tell you, even Solomon in all his royal splendor
    never wore a robe as rich as one of theirs.
Now if God gives such beautiful clothing to the grass
    — which is wilted and gone in a day —
how much more will He take care of you,
    in spite of your lack of faith?
So do not be concerned about your daily needs
    — that's the worry *pagans* have.

But you have a Father in heaven who knows your every need.
Set your hearts first and foremost on His Kingdom,
and everything else you need will come your way as well.

☆　　☆　　☆

CHORUS　*When Moses came down from Mount Sinai,*
all the people of Israel gathered around him.
And he passed on to them all the laws
that the Lord had given him on the Mount.
— *Exodus 34:29,32*

BLUEPRINTS FOR CHRISTIANS

A medieval humanist, on reading the Sermon on the Mount,
made the following comment:
"Either this is not Christianity, or we are not Christians!"
If that was his opinion then, what would he say today?
The sickness of our modern society was clearly spelled out
in one of the best sellers of 1977: *Looking Out for # 1.*
Compare the following excerpts from this book
with what Our Lord had to say in the Sermon on the Mount:

"But I say to you: If a man even look at a woman with lust,
he has already committed adultery with her in his heart."
　　"Eliminate all unsolicited moral opinions of others.
　　No other living person has the right to decide what
　　is moral (right or wrong) for you."
"If someone slaps you on the right cheek,
offer him the other one also."
　　"You needn't accept nagging or coercion for the sake of
　　keeping the peace. You have a right to live your life
　　as you please . . ."
"Treat others as you want them to treat you."
　　"Don't try to be all things to all people . . . You'll
　　never please everyone, so you'll only succeed
　　in frustrating yourself if you try."
"When you give money to someone in need, your left hand
should not know what your right hand is doing."
　　"Can you buy friendship? You not only can, you must.
　　It's the *only* way to obtain friends. Everything
　　worthwhile has a price."

"Love your enemies. Do good to those who hate you . . ."
"A crummy love relationship is one in which you
consistently give more than you receive."

☆   ☆   ☆

Some years ago the following message was printed
on a church's outdoor bulletin-board:
"If you were on trial for being a Christian,
would there be enough evidence to convict you?"
Before you answer, read Matthew, chapters 5, 6, and 7.

16

Jerusalem, a few months later. Near the main entrance to the Pool of Bethsaida, CROWDS are milling about.

Jn 5:1-47 / 10:30-39

Enter BEN-JUDAH, *a man in his 60's, carrying a rolled-up sleeping-mat on his back.* LEVI, *a scribe, and several* PHARISEES *approach him.*

LEVI
You old fool! Where are you going with that pack? You are breaking the Law! It's the Sabbath!

BEN-JUDAH
The man who just cured me told me: "Pick up your mat and walk."

LEVI
Someone cured you?

BEN-JUDAH
Yes! For 38 years I've been a helpless cripple.
Time and again I crawled here to Bethsaida,
hoping for a miracle whenever God moved the waters.
This morning a man approached me and asked:
"Do you want to get well?"
I explained I had no one to help me into the pool
when God stirred up the waters.
Someone was always there ahead of me.
He told me then: "Get up,
roll up your sleeping-mat, and leave."

LEVI
Who is it that said that to you?

BEN-JUDAH
I don't know, sir. He disappeared into the crowd
before I had a chance to . . . Wait!
There is is now — (*pointing*) by that portico!

LEVI
The Nazarene! (*to the* PHARISEES) Follow me!

(*They ascend the steps and approach* JESUS.)

Who gave you permission to break the Sabbath Law?

JESUS
My Father works on the Sabbath, and so do I.

59

LEVI	Your *father!* Only *God* can work on the Sabbath.
JESUS	I cannot do a thing on my own. I can do only what I see my Father doing. The Father shows me everything He does, so that whatever He does, I also can do. The Father is the Author of life, so is the Son. The Father brings the dead back to life, and so does the Son. The hour is already here, when the dead will hear the voice of the Son of God. The graves will open, the dead will rise: those who did good, will enter into life; those who did evil, will be condemned. The Father Himself judges no one; He has made the Son supreme judge, since he is the Son of Man. The Son is to receive the same honor that the Father receives. To dishonor the Son is to dishonor the Father who sent him.
LEVI	You're acting as your own witness. Such testimony is invalid.
JESUS	My testimony *is* valid, for I have *three* witnesses. First, there was John, whom you yourselves examined at the Jordan. John was only a lamp, shedding a pale light on the One who is Light Itself. Next, I have Moses as a witness. If you believed Moses, you would also believe me, since it was about *me* that he wrote. How ironic! You investigate the Scriptures, thinking that they will give you eternal life. Yet you refuse to come to me for life — the very one the Scriptures give witness to. And finally, the Father is my witness. The marvelous works that He gave me to do — these very works prove that the Father has sent me. The Father and I are one!

LEVI	For that we should stone you to death!
JESUS	I have done many good works in my Father's name. For which one are you going to stone me?
LEVI	We would stone you not for any good work, but for blasphemy! You're only a *man*, yet you make yourself out to be *God!*
JESUS	If I am not doing what my Father told me, you are right not to believe in me. But if I am doing His will, even if you refuse to believe in *me*, at least accept the works I do as proof that the Father is in me and I am in the Father.

JESUS *turns and exits with his* DISCIPLES.

☆　　☆　　☆

CHORUS	*Thus says the Lord God:* *"You will know that I am the Lord,* *when I open your graves, my people,* *and raise you from where you are buried."*

— Ezekiel 37:13

JESUS AND THE FATHER

In the entire O.T. God is called "Father" *only 14 times.*
Nine of those times God Himself is the speaker!
"If I am a father, then where is my honor?" (Ml 1:6)
In the Book of Psalms (a collection of 150 prayers)
not *once* is God addressed as "Father"!
Therefore, we may conclude:
The Jews considered God to be so far above them
that they avoided calling Him "Father".
But with Jesus, a strange thing happens:
He refers to God as "Father" *over 160 times!*
What's more, we have seven examples of how He prayed:
Mt 11:25 "I praise You, Father, Lord of heaven and earth . . ."
Mk 14:36 "Abba, Father, take this cup from me . . ."
Lk 23:34 "Father, forgive them, they know not what they do."

61

Lk 23:46 "Father, into Your hands I commend my spirit."
Jn 11:41 "Father, . . . I know that You always hear me . . ."
Jn 12:28 "Father, give glory to Your name . . ."
Jn 17:?? "Father, the hour has come. Glorify Your Son . . ."
How strange that an upright Jew would address God that way!
What was His relationship to God?
Merely that of an *adopted* son — like the rest of us?
Then why was He always so careful to distinguish between
"*My* Father" and "*your* Father" but never "*our* Father"?
(The Lords Prayer is *no* exception! He was teaching *us:*
"When *you* pray, say: '*Our* Father, who art in heaven' ". Lk 11:2)
Mark records the actual word Jesus used in prayer, "*Abba*".
But the usual word for "father" in Aramaic is "*ab*".
"*Abba*" was a term of affection (like "Dad" in English)
to be used only by a *natural* son in a family setting.
Then why did Jesus use it?
There is only one explanation possible:
He *is* God's natural Son!
Try to digest these three points:
LIKE BEGETS LIKE.
That means: cats give birth to cats, humans to humans.
And the offspring is as much a cat or a human as the parent.
Now if God had a Son — a *natural* Son —
the Son must be just as much *God* as the Father.
Like begets like!
"FATHER" AND "CHILD" ARE RECIPROCAL TERMS.
That is, you can't have *one* without the *other.*
(A husband is not a *father* until his *child* is conceived.)
Therefore, we can conclude:
If God has a natural *Son,* then God is also a *Father.*
You can't have one without the other!
GOD'S SON ALWAYS EXISTED.
For this part, turn to John 1:1-18 (the prologue).
Some of it sounds like a riddle, doesn't it?
What is St. John telling us? Five things, really:

1) *From all eternity God had a* CONCEPT *of Himself:*
   "In the beginning was the WORD." (v. 1)

2) "CONCEIVE" *is used in two ways:*
   a) to conceive a child in the *womb,*

b) to conceive an idea in the *mind.*

3) *Verse 18* COMBINES *both meanings of "conceive":*
"The WORD was in the presence of *God."* (v. 1)
"The only SON, who is near the *Father's* heart." (v. 18)

4) *Since God is Spirit, His act of fathering was* SPIRITUAL:
From all eternity God *knew* Himself.
From this self-knowledge came the *Word* — His only *Son.*

5) *God's Son took on our human nature* (= *the* INCARNATION).
"And the Word became flesh, and lived in our midst." (v. 14)

So there you have the divine riddle solved!
What was God's motive in sending His Son? Love.
"God so loved the world that He gave His only Son." (Jn 3:16)
And what must be our response? Faith.
"Whoever does not believe is already condemned
for refusing to believe in the only Son of God." (Jn 3:18)

17

Galilee, several weeks later. As the scene opens, a large crowd is in the process of dispersing, after listening to JESUS all afternoon. An EXPERT of the Law approaches him.

Mk 12:28-31 / Lk 10:25-37

LAW-
EXPERT

Rabbi, in your opinion,
which of the commandments is the most important?

JESUS

The first commandment is:
"Hear, O Israel, the Lord our God is Lord alone!
You are to love the Lord your God
with all your heart and soul,
with all your mind and strength."
And the sceond most important commandment is:
"You are to love your neighbor
as you love yourself."

LAW-
EXPERT

I see — but tell me —
exactly who is my neighbor?

JESUS

A man was on his way to Jericho
when he was attacked by robbers.
They took everything he had,
beat him senseless,
then left him there half-dead.
Along came a priest.
He stopped,
saw him,
then walked around him to get by.
Next, a Temple attendant came along.
He, too, saw him,
but continued on down the road.
Then a hated Samaritan happened to come by.
When he saw him,

he was overcome with emotion.
He went up to him,
soothed his wounds with oil and wine
and bandaged them.
Then he mounted him on his own donkey,
and brought him to an inn
where he took care of him that night.
In the morning, he took out two silver coins
and handed them to the innkeeper.
"Take care of him," he said, "until I return.
I shall then reimburse you for any other expenses."
Now, which one of these three would you say
was the neighbor of the man who had been robbed?

LAW-
EXPERT   I suppose it was the one who helped him.

JESUS   Yes. Now you must go and do the same.

☆   ☆   ☆

CHORUS   *Thus says the Lord of Hosts:*
"O Jerusalem, as I was passing by,
I saw you writhing in your own blood.
With some water I washed off your blood
and I soothed you with oil.
I dressed you in the finest robes,
and you became the queen of nations;
for I surrounded you with my own glory."
                    — *Ezekiel 16:6-14* (*passim*)

LOVE OUR ENEMIES?

Have you ever tasted *sweet* vinegar?
Of course not. It's a contradiction in terms.
Well, we've heard the words "a *good* Samaritan" so often
that we fail to realize that for the Jews of Jesus' day
a Samaritan was anything but good.
The Samaritans lived in central
  Palestine,
with the Jews to the north and south
  of them.
They were a race of half-breeds.
When the Jews had been taken into
  exile,
those who stayed behind, intermarried
with the despised gentile invaders.
On returning to their homeland,
the Jews had nothing but contempt
  for the new mixed-race.
So bitter was their mutual hatred,
  that:
1) there was no communication between them, (Jn 4:9)
2) no courtesy was expected from either side, (Lk 17:16-18)
3) to call a Jew "a Samaritan" was an insult. (Jn 8:48)
So when Jesus made a Samaritan the hero of His parable
to illustrate genuine love of neighbor,
the law-expert was so shocked
that he could not bring himself to pronounce
in a complimentary way the hated word "Samaritan".
That's why his reply to Jesus was: "The one who helped him."
(Imagine what a white-racist would have answered
on hearing a similar story, where the hero was a black.)
So if we are Christians, that is, followers of Christ,
our love must exclude no one.
"If anyone says he loves God, but hates his neighbor,
he is a liar.
For how can he love God whom he has never seen,
when he hates his neighbor whom he does see.
For this is the command that Jesus gave us:
the one who loves God must love his neighbor also." (1 Jn 4:20)

☆ ☆ ☆

The parable of the Good Samaritan also illustrates
the three main world systems, locked in mortal combat:
1. Communism (*the robbers*):   "What's yours is mine.
                                 I take it by force."
2. Capitalism* (*priest/levite*):   "What's mine is mine.
                                     I hoard it selfishly."
3. Christianity (*Samaritan*):   "What's mine is yours.
                                 I share it generously."

Like all of us,
the first Christians were keenly aware of what Jesus said:
"Do not store up your wealth here on earth,
where you can lose it to moths and rust and robbers.
Rather, store up your treasure in heaven,
where moths, rust, and robbers cannot touch it.
For wherever your treasure is,
your heart will be there, too." (Mt 6:19-21)
But unlike most of us,
the first Christians put Jesus' words into practice:
"Now all the believers shared everything they had.
They would sell their belongings
and distribute the money to those in need." (Ac 2:44,45)

---

* By this is meant, not *private property,* but rather the system of exploitative
Big Business, which accumulates unjust profits at the expense of the laboring
poor.

18

A week later. JESUS and the TWELVE have left Jewish territory and are nearing the coastal city of Tyre. A gentile WOMAN runs up to them.

Mt 15:21-28

WOMAN   (*shouting*) Son of David, help me!
I have a daughter who is possessed by a demon.
(JESUS *ignores her.*) Please pity me!
She's at the point of death.

(JESUS, *still ignoring her, continues walking.*
The WOMAN *continues her pleading.*)

PETER   (*approaching* JESUS) Send her away!
All that shouting is disturbing us.

JESUS   My main concern is with the lost sheep of Israel.

WOMAN   (*falling at his feet*) Please, sir, help me!

JESUS   It's not right to take the children's bread
and feed it to dogs.

WOMAN   How true, Rabbi!
But even the dogs eat the crumbs
that fall from their master's table.

JESUS   O woman, your faith is great, indeed!
Go — your prayer has been answered.
Your daughter is cured.

☆   ☆   ☆

CHORUS   *I cry to You, O Lord, my Rock.*
Do not turn a deaf ear to me.
If You are silent,
I shall go down to the grave like all flesh.
Hear my voice, as I cry out
and pray to You for help.

— Psalm 28:1,2

68

WHY PRAY?

At times people voice the complaint,
"God knows all our needs, so why pray?"
Consider the following case:
A father asks his sixteen-year-old son at supper,
"Steve, how did you do in the track-meet today?"
The boy continues eating.
The father repeats the question and is ignored a second time.
Who would tolerate such an attitude?
Yet very often that's how we treat God.
We ignore Him.
For God is constantly speaking to us
— in the rain and sunshine He sends on our crops,
— in the love that family and friends shower on us,
— in the gift of faith that brings salvation.
Like any loving parent, God expects us to answer Him.
That's what prayer is: speaking to God.
Let's return to the example of the teenager:
A healthy relationship with his father should include:
1. *Apology:* "I'm sorry, Dad. Please forget what I did."
2. *Praise:* "Happy birthday, Dad. You're Great!"
3. *Request:* "Dad, may I use the car tonight?"
4. *Thanks:* "I had a terrific time. Thanks, Dad."
All four elements form part of the Church's great prayer,

Holy Mass:
1. *Penitential rite:* "I confess to almighty God . . ."
2. *Gloria:* "We praise You, we bless You . . ."
3. *Oration:* "O God, guide us in Your ways . . ."
4. *Eucharistic prayer:* "Let us give thanks to the Lord . . ."
Too often our prayer is not sincere.
While we pray with our lips, "Thy Will be done",
in our hearts, we really want God to conform Himself to us.
We are like the youngster who one night asked God
to please make Paris the capital of Germany,
since that was the answer he had given on his test that day.
Contrast this attitude with that of Jesus,
our perfect model in prayer:

"Father, not my will, but Yours be done." (Mk 14:36)
Can you recall the last time you spent two minutes
alone in prayer to God?
"And he spent the whole night in prayer to God." (Lk 6:12)

19

A few weeks later, JESUS and the TWELVE approach the city of Caesarea Philippi. They pause to rest by the road.

Mt 16:13-28 / 20:17-19

JESUS   Who do people say I am?

PHILIP   Some people think you're John the Baptist.

ANDREW   And I heard some others say
that you're Elijah
or one of the prophets back from the dead.

JESUS   But in your opinion, who am I?

PETER   You are the Messiah — the Son of the living God!

JESUS   How blessed you are, Simon son of John!
For this was disclosed to you by none other
than my Father in heaven.
Now listen to what I tell you:
You are the Rock
and on this rock I will build my Church,
and the forces of Satan will never destroy it.
I will give you the keys to the Kingdom of heaven.
Whatever you forbid on earth
will be forbidden in heaven.
Whatever you permit on earth
will be permitted in heaven.

(*They continue on towards the town.*
JESUS *stops and turns again.*)

Now all of you, listen carefully to what I say.
You are to tell no one who I am
until I have risen from the dead.
Before then, however, we must go up to Jerusalem,
where I shall be given up to the Chief Priests.

71

	They, in turn, will hand me over to the Romans,
	to be mocked and whipped and crucified.
	Then on the third day, I shall rise again.
PETER	(*pulling* JESUS *aside*) God forbid!
	That will never happen to you!
JESUS	Get away from me, you Satan!

PETER   (*pulling* JESUS *aside*) God forbid!
           That will never happen to you!

JESUS   Get away from me, you Satan!
           For you don't have the interests of God at heart,
           but those of worldly men.
           Now, all of you, listen again.
           Anyone who wants to be my disciple
           must say "No" to himself,
           shoulder his cross day after day,
           and follow me.
           If you think only of yourself,
           you will be lost.
           But if you forget yourself for my sake,
           you will be saved.
           For what good will it do you
           to become master of the whole world,
           and then lose your immortal soul?

                     ☆   ☆   ☆

CHORUS   *Behold, I am placing a stone in Zion,*
           a rock of witness,
           a precious cornerstone for a strong foundation . . .
           I will give him the key of the House of David:
           Whatever he opens, no one will shut.
           Whatever he shuts, no one will open.
                                    — Isaiah 28:16/22:22

A MAN CALLED ROCK

Who has the oldest government in the world today?
The United States? Switzerland? England?
Guess again. It's the Roman Catholic Church.
("Catholic" means that it's world-wide. (Rm 1:8)
"Roman" means that the Bishop of *Rome* is its leader.)
The present head, Pope John Paul, took over in 1978 . . .
Pius X in 1903 . . . Gregory VII in 1073 . . . Leo I in 440 . . .

all the way back to the Apostle Simon Peter in 30 A.D.!
(He first brought the faith to Rome around 42 A.D.)
You say, "Why get worked up about that?"
Let's look at it this way:
In the Old Testament,
God Himself hand-picked one leader
to be His representative among His chosen people.
Take Moses, for example. He wasn't the people's choice.
They often complained:
"Why did you lead us out of Egypt?" (Ex 17:3)
Time and again he had to tear them away from idol-worship
and redirect their steps towards the Promised Land.
Later, God sent prophets to speak in His name:
"Listen, I am putting *My* words on *your* lips . . ." (Jr 1:9)
In the New Testament, we see the process repeated:
Jesus selected *one* man to represent Him —
Simon the fisherman.
The first time He set eyes on him, Jesus changed his name:
"You are Simon . . . You will be called the ROCK." (Jn 1:42)
To the Jews a NAME (*Abraham:* father of a great people)
was like a NICKNAME (*Stonewall* Jackson / *Buffalo* Bill):
it spelled out a person's MAIN ROLE in life.
Why, then, was Simon renamed "the ROCK?"
What job did Jesus have in mind for him?
He gives us the answer in Mt 16:18-19.

Let's analyze it:
"You are the ROCK": the only time Jesus calls him the ROCK!
   (In the O.T. only God was given that title:
     "Who else is a ROCK except our God?" — Ps 18:31)
"and on this rock I will build my Church": not "ChurchES"!
"and the forces of Satan will never destroy it": Why not?
For the answer, turn to Mt 7:24-27:
   One man builds a house on rock, another on sand.
   Along comes a hurricane and demolishes the second house.
   The other remains standing "because it is built on *rock.*"
Why will the Church which Jesus established never collapse?
Because He built it on the ROCK — Simon Peter!
Like a foundation which must *support* an entire building,
Simon is to strengthen all others in the faith. (Lk 22:32)

"I will give you the keys of the Kingdom of Heaven"
Keys stand for authority.
If your dad gives you the keys to the family car,
you are the one who decides where to take it tonight.
"Whatever you forbid / permit on EARTH . . ."
Simon is to exercise his authority ("keys")
as the Lord's VISIBLE representative ("on earth").
". . . will be forbidden / permitted in HEAVEN."
After His return to heaven, Jesus promises to confirm
whatever Simon has decided here on earth!
Like Moses — God's representative to the Israelites —
Simon must now speak in God's name to the New Israel
as she resists the attacks of her Satanic Pharoah. (Rv 20:9)
At times, the Israelites of old rebelled in the desert:
"What has become of this Moses?" (Ex 32:1)
Likewise, there have been times when the new Israel
rejected the successor of Peter
and worshipped the golden calf of this world.
But there was the Rock — the Holy Father in Rome —
still speaking in the name of Jesus.

☆　　☆　　☆

Q. *Doesn't Peter as the foundation contradict 1 Co 3:11,*
   "No other foundation can be laid except . . . Jesus Christ?"
A. Jesus *is* the Church's only foundation, but INVISIBLE.
   He Himself made Peter His VISIBLE representative.
   On earth He had often linked Himself *only with Peter:*
   1) He used Peter's boat. (Lk 5:3)
   2) Only He and Peter walked on the water. (Mt 14:29)
   3) Only He and Peter paid the temple-tax (Mt 17:27)
   4) Only He and Peter were called "the ROCK"! (1 Co 10:4)

20

It is late one afternoon in early spring. JESUS has been preaching to a CROWD of 5,000 on the slope of a hill on the eastern shore of the Sea of Galilee.

Jn 6:1-21

JESUS   Philip, where can we buy some bread
to feed these people?

PHILIP   Buy some bread?
Why, 200 silver coins wouldn't buy enough bread
to give each one even a small piece.

ANDREW   (*leading a young lad by the arm*)
This little boy
has five loaves of barley bread and two dried fish.
But what is that for such a large crowd?

JESUS has ANDREW hold out his tunic apron-fashion. He takes the bread, looks up to heaven, and prays a moment in silence. He places the loaves in ANDREW'S tunic, which immediately fills with bread. He does the same with the fish. The process is repeated with the other DISCIPLES.

JESUS   Now go out through the crowd
and give everyone as much as he wants.

(*The DISCIPLES do so. As they return, everyone is eating contentedly.*)

Go back now and gather what is left
so that nothing is wasted.

In minutes the DISCIPLES have returned with their tunics overflowing with leftovers. Suddenly SOMEONE stands up in the crowd.

1st MAN   Our long-awaited Prophet is here at last!

75

2nd MAN	He must be the Messiah for sure!
3rd MAN	Halleluia! Let's make him king!

As the crowd begins to chant "Long live the King!"
JESUS turns and goes up the hill alone. The
TWELVE head for SIMON'S boat moored on the shore.

☆   ☆   ☆

CHORUS　　*Moses said to the people:*
"This is the bread that the Lord has given you.
You are to gather as much of it as you need."
The Israelites called the bread "manna".
They ate it for the next forty years
until they reached the Promised Land.

—Exodus 16:15,16,31,35

GOD SETS A TABLE FOR 5,000

Can a clockmaker make his clock run backwards?
Of course he can.
He simply readjusts a few wheels to reverse its direction.
What we moderns grant to a simple clockmaker
we deny to almighty God.
For we say that miracles are impossible.
What we're really saying is that the Divine Lawmaker
cannot reverse the very laws of nature that He Himself made.
In our efforts to make everything reasonable,
we draw the most unreasonable conclusions.
For some say that Jesus did not really multiply the loaves.
You see, everyone had brought his own lunch along;
but not wishing to share it with anyone else,
he was keeping it under cover until he could eat it alone.
The good example of the boy's sharing his lunch with Jesus
prompted all the people to share their food, too.
The "miracle" was that Jesus inspired them to be generous.
Such an explanation makes a colossal liar of St. John,
since he reported the following items as factual:
1) Philip's problem with financing such an enormous meal,
2) Andrew's remark about the futility of 5 loaves for 5,000,
3) Jesus' solemn blessing of the 5 loaves,

76

4) the 12 baskets of leftovers that were collected,
5) the crowd's attempt to force Jesus to be their king.
But more at issue, denying this miracle
disrupts the three-part unity of John's sixth chapter.

PART I: By feeding the 5,000 with just 5 loaves of bread,
Jesus suspended the process
that begins with spring planting and ends in an oven
— a process that requires many months and much effort.
With His blessing, Jesus was proclaiming:
"I can bypass the natural order for BREAD."

PART II: That night while the disciples were struggling
to steer their boat on the storm-swept sea,
Jesus came walking towards them on the surface of the water.
At first glance, this miracle seems to be pointless.
What was Jesus trying to prove by it?
According to the law of gravity
all bodies must seek their rest on the earth's surface.
By preventing His body from sinking, Jesus was saying:
"I can bypass the physical order for my BODY."

PART III: The next day the Jews who had eaten of the loaves
came to Jesus on the other side of the lake to make him king.
Jesus used the occasion to teach them that one day
He would give them a special BREAD that would be His BODY.
In making this extraordinary promise, He was merely
drawing the logical conclusion from the first two parts:
1) "I can do what I want with BREAD."
2) "I can do what I want with my BODY."
3) "The BREAD that I will give is my BODY." (Jn 6:51)
Our objective for the next section
is to study Part III in greater detail:
Jesus is the BREAD OF LIFE.

21 The next afternoon in the synagogue at Capernaum. JESUS has finished an instruction. Enter a SEGMENT of the crowd that ate the miraculous loaves of the previous day.

Jn 6:22-71

1st MAN   Rabbi, how did you come here?

JESUS   You are looking for me
not because you understood the miracle,
but because you had your fill of bread.
Do not yearn for food that spoils.
Rather, seek the food that lasts forever —
the very food that I myself will give you.

1st MAN   We would like to see some specific proof,
like the manna from heaven
that our fathers ate in the desert.

JESUS   Moses never gave you bread from heaven.
It is my Father who gives you real heavenly bread.
That bread is none other
than the one who comes down from heaven
and gives life to the world.

2nd MAN   Rabbi, please give us that bread.

JESUS   I myself am that life-giving bread.
I have come down from heaven
to do only what my Father wants.
And what He wants is this:
that on the last day I should bring back to life
everyone who has believed in me.

1st MAN   (*aside*) What kind of talk is that?

78

2nd MAN	I don't know.
	He's only the son of a carpenter.
3rd MAN	Then how can he say that he came down from heaven?
JESUS	Stop your murmuring.
	Your fathers ate manna in the desert,
	but they died.
	Whoever eats the bread that comes from heaven
	will never die.
	I myself am that living bread from heaven.
	If anyone eats this bread,
	he will live forever.
	And the bread that I will give is my own body
	to impart life to the world.
3rd MAN	(*aside*) Incredible!
	How can he give us his body to eat?
JESUS	I am telling you the truth.
	If you do not eat my body and drink my blood,
	you will have no life in you.
	For my body is real food,
	and my blood is real drink.
	Just as my life comes from the Father,
	so too, the one who eats me
	will receive life from me.
	Whoever eats my body and drinks my blood
	will have divine life in him,
	and I will raise him up on the last day.
	This is the bread that came down from heaven.
	The one who eats this bread will live forever.
1st MAN	What madness!
	How can anyone pay any attention to him?
	Let's get away from here.
	Exit a large GROUP, *including many* DISCIPLES.
JESUS	(*to the* TWELVE) Do you want to leave me, too?
PETER	Lord, to whom can we go?
	You alone have words that give divine life.
	Besides, we know that you are God's holy one.

☆　☆　☆

CHORUS　　*He opened the doors of heaven
and rained down manna on them to eat.
He sent them food from heaven,
and men ate the bread of angels.*

— Psalm 78:23-25

LIFE-GIVING BREAD

All living things — plants, animals, and man —
need food to survive.
Furthermore, each species needs its own appropriate food.
For example, cows cannot eat meat; man will starve on hay.
So in giving us His divine life at baptism,
Jesus also promised a special food to nourish that life —
His own body and blood (the Eucharist).
"If you do not eat the flesh of the Son of Man
and drink His blood,
you will have no life in you." (Jn 6:53)
When did Jesus fulfill that promise?
At the last supper, when He blessed the bread and wine:
"Eat. This is my body . . . Drink. This is my blood."
For 2,000 years this has been the Church's teaching:
At Mass when the priest repeats what Jesus said,
the bread is completely changed into His body
and the wine is completely changed into His blood,
even though they still look the same.
Does this seem incredible?
Then compare it with the following example.
You grasp an iron bar.
How do you know that it is iron?
From its weight, hardness, and color.
But in outer space the bar loses its weight,
and in a blast furnace it becomes a red-hot liquid.
Is it still iron?
Yes, for its *substance* remains the same;
only its *accidentals* (weight, hardness, color) have changed.
In the blast furnace of God's love at Mass,
the direct opposite takes place:
the *accidentals* of the bread and wine remain the same,
the *substance* changes into the Lord's own body and blood.
(This marvelous change is called *transubstantiation*.)
Ever since that afternoon of the promise at Capernaum,
men have refused to take Jesus at His word.
Some have said that the Eucharist only *represents* Him
just as the stars and stripes represent our country.

However, someone who burns our country's flag
is charged with desecrating our *flag,* not our country.
But in 1 Co 11:27, St. Paul says emphatically:
"Whoever eats this bread or drinks the Lord's cup unworthily
will be guilty of desecrating the Lord's *body* and *blood."*
Besides, if Jesus meant a mere symbolic eating of His flesh,
why did He allow His listeners to take Him so literally?
Elsewhere in John, when Jesus' listeners misunderstood Him,
the misunderstanding was corrected at once:
Jn 2:21 The temple to be raised up in three days
    was Jesus' *body,* not the Jewish Temple of stone.
Jn 3:5 When Nicodemus understood a physical rebirth,
    Jesus pointed out that He had meant a *spiritual* one.
Jn 11:13 When the disciples thought Lazarus was asleep,
    Jesus said plainly that He had meant the sleep of *death.*
But when His listeners at Capernaum objected,
"How can this man give us his flesh to eat?" (Jn 6:52),
far from correcting them,
Jesus went on to reinforce His statement by adding
that they must also drink His blood! (v. 53)
When they refused to accept this "intolerable teaching",
Jesus knowingly let them walk off.
If He had intended only a symbolic eating of His flesh:
why did He not correct the misunderstanding? (v. 52)
why did He allow His disciples to desert Him? (v. 66)
why did He ask the twelve if they were leaving? (v. 67)
The obvious answer is
that He wanted to be understood literally!
1) "I can do what I want with BREAD." (v. 11)
2) "I can do what I want with my BODY." (v. 19)
3) "The BREAD that I will give is my BODY
    for the life of the world." (v. 51)

22

Capernaum, several months later. JESUS and his DISCIPLES are having dinner in the home of SIMON the Pharisee.

Lk 7:36-50 / 15:11-32

As ALL *are reclining at table and helping them-*selves from the common bowl in the center, a WOMAN *enters with a jar of perfume and scans the faces of the* GUESTS.

SCRIBE   (*aside*) Simon, look at what just walked in!

SIMON P. O no! The town slut!
     And she's throwing herself at the Rabbi's feet!

SCRIBE   (*aside*) Incredible! She's kissing his feet!
     And look at her now — smearing them with perfume!

     The GUESTS' *stunned silence is broken by the* WOMAN'S *loud sobbing.*

SIMON P. That man is no prophet.
     If he were, he'd know what sort of woman she is
     and would never let her near him.

JESUS   Simon, I have something to tell you.

SIMON P. By all means, Rabbi.

JESUS   There once was a man who had two sons.
     One day the younger son said to his father:
     "I want my share of the property now!"
     So the father gave it to him.
     A few days later the boy packed up
     and went to another country
     where he spent all his money on wine and women.
     When he was left without a penny,
     he went to work on a farm, taking care of pigs.
     He was so hungry,
     that he wanted to eat the garbage

that the pigs were wallowing in.
At last he came to his senses and said:
"To think that all my father's hired hands
have more than they can eat,
while I'm about to starve!
I will return to my father and tell him:
'Father, I've wronged both God and you.
I'm not fit to be your son any more.
Please take me back as one of your workers.'"
So he started for home.
He was still a long way off
when his father caught sight of him.
Overcome with emotion, he ran out to meet him,
and welcomed him with tears of joy.
His son said: "Dad, I've wronged both God and you.
I'm not fit to be your son. Make me . . ."
But his father called out to the servants:
"Quick!! Bring my best coat and put it on him!
Put a ring on his finger and shoes on his feet!
Get our finest calf and kill it!
We're going to celebrate!
For my boy was dead — but now he's alive!
He was lost — but now he's back again!"
And they began to celebrate.
Meantime, the other son was out in the fields.
As he came in from work,
he could hear the party songs and dancing.
So he asked a servant what was going on.
The servant told him: "Your brother is back!
And your father killed the prize calf
to celebrate his safe return!" —
He became so furious, he refused to go in.
So his father came out to plead with him.
But he snapped at him:
"Look!! All these years I've slaved for you,
doing every single thing you asked me.
Yet what did you ever give *me?*
Not even a *scrawny goat*
so that I could have my friends in for a party.

But when this son of yours turns up —
after spending all your money on his women —
for *him* you kill the *finest calf* we had!!"
The father answered:
"My son, you are here with me always,
and everything I have is yours.
But we had to celebrate this happy occasion.
Remember, he is still your brother.
He was dead — but now he's alive!
He was lost — but now he's back again!" —
Now then, Simon, in your opinion,
which of the two sons will love his father more?

SIMON P. The younger one, I suppose, since he was forgiven.

JESUS Exactly.
Do you see this woman, Simon?
When I came into your house,
you provided no water for my feet;
she has washed them with her tears.
You did not welcome me with the customary kiss;
she has not stopped kissing my feet for a moment.
You failed to anoint my head with oil;
she has anointed my feet with perfume.
And so I tell you,
her many sins have been forgiven
because she has shown such great love.
(*to the* WOMAN) Go, your sins are forgiven.

SCRIBE (*aside*) Who can this man be?
He even forgives sins!

CHORUS *Though your sins are red as scarlet, says the Lord,*
I will make them as white as snow.

— *Isaiah 1:18*

TO FORGIVE IS DIVINE

One day Peter asked the Lord,
"How many times should I forgive someone who offends me?
Up to seven times? (Mt 18:21)

Jesus answered, "Not seven times, but seventy times seven."
With that reply Jesus gave the hallmark of a Christian:
Forgiveness.
So important did Jesus consider this duty that He placed it
on a higher level than offering gifts to God:
"If you're about to offer God a gift at the altar,
and there you recall some offense against your brother,
leave your gift at the altar,
go at once to make peace with your brother,
and then return to offer your gift to God." (Mt 5:23,24)
In praying the Lord's prayer, we condemn ourselves
every time that we refuse to forgive others:
"Forgive us our offences
just as we forgive those who have offended us."
With His dying lips Jesus even forgave His executioners:
"Father, forgive them; they don't know what they're doing."
The parable of the Prodigal Son is a masterpiece.
The father — so ready to forgive — represents God.
The sulking older brother stands for our unforgiving selves.
Like Simon the Pharisee, we humans often judge others
as unworthy of forgiveness.
The younger son represents those guilty of sins of the FLESH:
heavy drinking, drugs, illicit sex.
Many teenagers are lured by these "instant pleasures".
Like the younger son, they crave "freedom" —
and sink down to the pig-pen!
When they again become God's "slaves" —
they are raised up to the banquet table!
The older brother embodies the sins of the SPIRIT:
anger: "He was so angry that he would not go in."
pride: "Never once have I disobeyed you."
resentment: "for *me* not even a kid goat"
hatred: "this son of yours" (disowning him as brother)
uncharity: "after spending all your money on prostitutes"
jealousy: "For *him* you kill the fattened calf."
Who could endure such a disposition?
Yet, sad to say,
such is the disposition of many "exemplary" Christians.
By an unforgiving attitude, we keep many a prodigal

craving spiritual food, far from his Father's house.
If you wish to examine yourself
to see if you are developing the attitude of the older son,
turn to First Corinthians, chapter 13.
Starting with verse 4 ("Love is patient, love is kind . . ."),
substitute your own name in place of the word "love".
If you can apply to yourself the twelve qualities of love,
then you can truly say you are like the forgiving father,
and not like the unforgiving older brother.

23

A street in Capernaum, a week later. As JESUS AND HIS DISCIPLES walk along, they are approached by a very wealthy YOUNG MAN.

Mk 10:17-27 / Lk 16:19-31

RICH MAN   Rabbi, what must I do to be saved?

JESUS   You know the commandments:
               "Do not kill.
               Do not commit adultery.
               Do not steal.
               Do not tell lies.
               Honor your father and your mother."
               Keep these commandments and you shall be saved.

RICH MAN   But I've kept them all ever since I was a child.

JESUS   There's only one thing left for you, then.
               Go, sell whatever you have
               and give the money to the poor.
               Then come, be my disciple,
               and you will have riches in heaven.

               (*The* YOUNG MAN *looks downcast, shakes his head
               slowly, turns without a word, and walks off.*
               JESUS *addresses his* DISCIPLES.)
               How difficult it is for the rich to be saved!
               It is easier for a camel
               to go through the eye of a needle
               than for a rich man to get into heaven.

JUDAS   Then who can be saved?

JESUS   Man cannot be saved on his own.
               But with God's help all things are possible.
               Now listen to this story, all of you.
               There was once a very wealthy man,

89

who was always dressed in imported garments
and ate nothing but the finest foods.
There was also a poor beggar named Lazarus,
lying in front of the rich man's gate.
He was covered with running sores,
which the dogs came up and licked.
He craved to eat the scraps of food
that fell from the rich man's table.
One day the beggar died
and was carried off by angels to rest with Abraham.
The rich man also died and had a grand funeral.
Suffering miserably in hell,
he looked up and saw Abraham a long way off
with Lazarus resting peacefully next to him.
"Father Abraham," he called out, "have some pity!
Send Lazarus to dip his finger in some water
and cool my tongue, for this fire is torturing me."
"My son," replied Abraham,
recall the life of ease you had on earth,
while Lazarus had nothing but hardships.
Now he is being rewarded, while you must suffer.
Furthermore, there's a huge chasm separating us,
that makes it impossible to cross over either way."
The rich man continued: "Then, father Abraham,
please send Lazarus to warn my five brothers
so that they can escape this fate."
Abraham said: "Your brothers have God's word.
They should pay attention to what it says."
"It's not enough, father Abraham!" he pleaded.
"But if someone were to come back from the dead,
then they would change their sinful ways."
Abraham answered:
"If they won't pay attention to God's word,
they won't be convinced
even if someone rises from the dead."

☆　　☆　　☆

CHORUS　　*Do not be troubled when a man becomes rich,*
when his possessions continue to grow.

For he can take nothing with him when he dies,
his wealth will not accompany him to the grave.
— Psalm 49:16,17

IS HELL FOR KEEPS?

C. S. Lewis once wrote
that if he could change one of the Church's teachings,
that teaching would be the doctrine of hell.
He would still have a hell, mind you,
but not one that would last forever.
Many people today refuse to believe in an eternal hell.
Their reasoning runs something like this:
"An all-merciful God would never punish someone *forever*
for a sin — no matter how serious —
that was committed in a short period of time.
After death, we'll be punished for a while — until purified,
but then we'll all be taken up into heaven."
Sounds reasonable, doesn't it?
And so compassionate!
But is it valid?
And will such a belief change reality?
Six centures ago everyone thought that the world was flat.
Did their belief flatten the globe?
Suppose we all refused to believe in an eternal hell.
Would our belief change the nature of hell?
Therefore, it's essential in a matter so basic
not to be misguided by any wishful thinking.
Our eternity depends on it!
In the Gospels Jesus mentions hell over a dozen times —
and always as a state of punishment that lasts *forever:*
Mt 25:41 "Depart, you cursed, into everlasting fire . . ."
Mk 9:48 "In hell, their worms will never die
                 and the scorching fire will never be quenched."
If the Lord were not serious about this matter,
why did He speak of it so often and so forcefully?
If hell is not the fearful reality He spoke of,
why, then, the Incarnation?
From what was God's Son saving us?

Our faith teaches:
1) God wants everyone to be saved. (1 Tm 2:4)
2) God gives us sufficient grace to be saved. (2 Co 12:9)
3) No one will be lost except though his own fault.
God does not reject the sinner;
it's the sinner who rejects God.
Yet in spite of all that God has done,
Jesus implies that many, many people will be lost:
"Enter by the narrow gate.
For the gate is wide and the road easy that leads to hell,
and there are many who go that way.
The gate is narrow and the road hard that leads to life,
and there are only a few who find it." (Mt 7:13)
To direct us along that narrow road leading to life
God placed ten road signs — the TEN COMMANDMENTS.
Some people complain that the commandments are too negative.
If a mountain road has been washed away,
would we accuse the trooper of being "negative"
for posting a detour sign?
For the rich young man Jesus listed only those commandments
that deal with our neighbor.
The full list of commandments is found in Ex 20:1-17.
We can paraphrase them as follows:
 1. Always put God first in your life.
 2. Never misuse God's name.
 3. Sanctify the Lord's day. (Mass and rest)
 4. Respect your parents and elders.
 5. Don't murder, fight, or hate.
 6. Avoid all illicit sex.
 7. Don't steal.
 8. Don't lie.
 9. Avoid impure thoughts and desires.
10. Don't crave what belongs to others.

24

Capernaum, two months later. The CROWDS are just dispersing after JESUS has finished instructing them. A group of PHARISEES approaches.

Mt 19:3-12 / Mk 10:10-12

PHARISEE   Rabbi, how serious a reason must a man have
to legally divorce his wife?

JESUS   Aren't you aware that from the very beginning
God made them male and female?
"And that's why a man must leave his parents,
unite with his wife,
and the two shall become one body."
Husband and wife, then, are no longer two,
but *one* body.
And so what God has joined as one,
let no man dare to separate.

PHARISEE   Then why did Moses say we could divorce?
In Deuteronomy he states quite plainly:
"If a man finds some fault with his wife,
he may give her a written divorce notice
and send her away."

JESUS   It was because you are so crass
that Moses allowed you to divorce your wives.
But it was never intended to be that way.
Now this is how it must be:
Anyone who divorces his wife and remarries
commits adultery.
And a divorcee who marries another man
also commits adultery.

PHARISEES *walk off shaking their heads in disbelief.*

93

PETER	Lord, if that's the way it is with marriage, it's better not to marry.
JESUS	Continence is not meant for everyone — it is a special gift from God. Some men are born incapable of marriage, others become that way through a malicious attack, and still others refrain from marriage to show their love for God. Whoever can follow this teaching, should do so.

☆   ☆   ☆

CHORUS	*Then Tobias got up from bed and prayed:* *O God of our fathers,* *You created Adam and his wife Eve,* *and from them the human race has come.* *It was You who said:* *"It is not good for man to be alone,* *let us make him a partner like himself."* *And so I do not take my bride out of lust,* *but rather, in purity of heart.* *Be kind to her and to me,* *and bring us together to a happy old age."*

— Tobit 8:7-9

"UNTIL DEATH DO US PART"

God does not make mistakes.
Marriage was part of His plan from the beginning:
"It is not good for man to be alone.
Let us make him a partner like himself." (Gn 2:18)
In choosing Israel as His people, God made a pact with her:
"The Lord our God made a covenant with us at Sinai." (Dt 5:2)
He modeled this pact on the marriage covenant:
"O Jerusalem, like a young man taking a bride,
your Maker will marry you." (Is 62:5)
By worshipping false gods, Israel became an adultress:
"Rejecting God, they play the whore with idols." (Hos 4:12)
Jesus compared His relationship with us to a marriage:
"The Kingdom of God is like a wedding feast

that a King gave His Son . . ." (Mt 22:2)
He began His public ministry at a wedding banquet:
"This first sign Jesus performed at Cana in Galilee." (Jn 2:11)
His final triumph is pictured as a grand wedding:
"Come and I will show you the bride of the Lamb." (Rv 21:9)
At times He referred to Himself as a husband:
"Can the wedding guests fast
while the bridegroom is still with them?" (Mk 2:19)
His bride is the Church:
"Husbands, love your wives as Christ loved the Church." (Eph 5:25)
But Christ's marriage is permanent:
"This is the cup of my blood
of the new and everlasting covenant." (Consecration at Mass)
For a time God had tolerated divorce under Moses:
"If a man should find some fault with his wife,
he may give her a divorce certificate . . ." (Dt 24:1)
But God still made it clear that divorce was evil:
"I hate divorce, says the Lord of Hosts." (Mal 2:16)
For Jesus divorce is not like separating lock and key:
"They are no longer two . . ."
Rather, it's like tearing out a heart from a living body:
". . . but they are one flesh." (Mt 19:5)
So a Christian marriage can never be dissolved by divorce:
"For those who are married I have this command
— it is not mine but the Lord's:
A wife must not leave her husband;
but if she does, she must either remain single,
or go back to her husband.
And a husband must not divorce his wife." (1 Co 7:10,11)
So when you stand before that altar and promise:
". . . until death do us part",
*the Church only wants you to be true
to what everyone in love already knows:*
"I'll love you till I die." (popular song)
And the ultimate measure of all true love is sacrifice:
"Christ loved her and gave Himself up for her." (Eph 5:25)

☆   ☆   ☆

So the Church doesn't look down on marriage.
On the contrary, she considers married love so precious

95

that she insists her priests, brothers, and sisters
make an offering of it to God
as our finest gift to Him:
"And there are eunuchs who have made themselves so
for the sake of the Kingdom of Heaven." (Mt 19:12)

25

Late that afternoon. House of Simon Peter's in-laws in Capernaum. Enter JESUS and his DISCIPLES. JESUS sits down opposite the door.

Mk 9:33-37; 10:13-16 / Mt 18:1-10; 10:29; 11:25-27

JESUS   Simon, what were you arguing about along the road?

Embarrassed, PETER *looks down at the floor.*

JAMES   (*aside*) John, do you suppose he overheard
our discussion about who's the greatest?

Suddenly, loud commotion at the door.
All heads turn in that direction.

THOMAS   (*trying to force the door shut*)
I said NOT NOW! He's too tired!
Besides, we haven't eaten since yesterday.

WOMAN   (*outside*) We won't be but a minute —
just long enough for him to bless our little ones.

THOMAS   Tomorrow, woman, tomorrow! I said he's . . .

JESUS   Let the little children come to me.
Do not stop them. For the Kingdom of God
belongs to those who are like them.

(*Enter three* WOMEN *with a group of* CHILDREN.
JESUS *takes a small child on his lap.*
He looks around at his DISCIPLES.)

Unless you change and become like little children,
you will have no place in the Kingdom of Heaven.
And if you want to know
who the greatest in that Kingdom is,
it's the one who humbles himself
and becomes like this little child.

Whoever helps one of these little ones in my name
is really helping me.
But if anyone teaches a child like this to sin,
that person should be thrown into the sea
with a millstone tied around his neck.

JOHN   Lord, why such preoccupation with little children?

JESUS   Two sparrows sell for just a penny,
yet not one of them falls to the ground
unless your Father in heaven allows it.
So too, your heavenly Father does not want
even one of these little ones to be lost.
For each one of them has an angel in heaven
who is always standing in my Father's presence.
(*He gathers the* CHILDREN *around him, and places his
hands on them. He then raises his eyes to heaven.*)
Father, Lord of heaven and earth,
I thank You for hiding Your truth
from those who think they are wise and learned
and for revealing it to little children.
Yes, Father, that is the way You wanted it.
I have received everything from my Father.
Only the Father knows the Son,
only the Son knows the Father,
and the Son shares this knowledge
with those he chooses.

☆   ☆   ☆

CHORUS   *O Lord our God,
You have trained little children
to offer perfect praise
in order to shame the mighty.*

— Psalm 8:1,2

THE WAR ON THE WOMB

"Let the little children come to me . . ." (Mk 10:14)
The Bible considers children a blessing. (Ps 127:3)
Barrenness is always a curse:
After Rachel had conceived, she said:

98

"God has taken away my disgrace." (Gn 30:23)
But we moderns consider children:
  a risk to be avoided: "Did you have an accident?"
  an enemy to be fought: "Would ruin my career!"
  an epidemic to be wiped out: "Too many people already!"
The main weapon for fighting children is *contraception.*
("Birth control," Chesterton once said, is a colossal
misnomer, since there is no *birth* and no *control.*")
Artificial contraception is always wrong:
1. *It's against God's Word:*
  "But everytime Onan had relations with his wife,
  he spilt his seed on the ground,
  to avoid providing a child for his brother.
  What he did was *evil* in the Lord's sight . . ." (Gn 38:9)*
2. *It's against Church teaching:*
  "Any act, either before or during marital relations,
  which tries to prevent the handing on of life,
  must be rejected." (Pope Paul, *Humanae Vitae,* #14)
3. *It's abnormal:*
  a) Is it normal for a wife to insert *ear-plugs,*
     while listening to her husband?
  b) Is it normal for a husband to *muffle his mouth,*
     while speaking to his wife?
  c) Is it proper for husband or wife to *tell a lie,*
     when the other requests legitimate information?
Then why during *sexual communication* do we tolerate:
  a) a wife wearing a *diaphragm,*
  b) a husband using a *condom,*
  c) a wife on the *pill* or a husband *withdrawing?*
(If you think this comparison is farfetched,
check out the word "intercourse" in Webster's:
What's its *first* meaning? What's its *second?*)
Someone may object:
"But sex isn't meant only for having children.
It's also a way to express love."

---

* In his encyclical *Casti Connubii,* Pius XI interpreted this text as a con-
demnation of artificial contraception. (Denz 2239). Modern scripture scholars
feel that Onan was punished because he refused to fulfill his duty as brother-
in-law. But the punishment for such a person is minutely described in Dt. 25:
7-10, which is a far cry from the death penalty inflicted on Onan.

99

True! God Himself planned sexuality that way:
1. *love-giving:* "A man shall unite with his wife"
2. *life-giving:* "the two shall become one flesh." (Gn 2:24)
These are really two faces of the same coin.
When you deliberately try to separate them,
then it's *lust* you're expressing, not *love.*
Sound modern psychiatry agrees. Dr. Viktor Frankl says:
"Pleasure is, and must remain,
a side effect or by-product (of sex),
and is destroyed and spoiled to the degree
to which it is made an end in itself."*
Gandhi, the father of modern India, once said:
"Self-control is the only method of regulating births.
Contraceptives are an insult to womanhood.
The only difference between a prostitute
and a woman using contraceptives,
is that the former sells her body to several men,
the latter sells it to one man." (*Harijan,* 5/5/46)
So if it's necessary to avoid conception,
the couple must use a moral method to do so —
Natural Family Planning (N.F.P.):
 A woman is fertile only a short time each month.
 During that period the couple abstains from relations.
 N.F.P. helps to determine the day of ovulation.**
"So what's the difference?
Seems to be the same as using an artificial means."
That's like saying: "Maintaining silence (=*abstaining*)
is the same thing as telling a lie (=*contraceptives*).
Besides, in N.F.P. God is still the Author of Life.
If He should send a child,
the couple using N.F.P. will welcome it;
the couple using an artificial means
may be tempted to abort it.
After all, when you've declared war on the womb,
you don't stop shooting at the enemy
once he crosses the front lines!

---

* *Man's Search for Meaning,* PocketBooks (N.Y. 1963), p. 194.
** For more information on N.F.P., write to: Couple to Couple League / Box 11084 / Cincinnati, OH 45211.

—Paul Conrad of the **Los Angeles Times**

26

Jerusalem, two months later. JESUS and his DISCIPLES are at prayer in the Temple. Enter a group of PHARISEES, dragging a WOMAN behind them.

Jn 8:1-11

PHARISEE   Rabbi, look at this woman!

(*He pushes her forward.*)

We just caught her sleeping with another man! Our Law commands her type to be stoned to death. Do you agree?

JESUS *circles the crowd slowly with his eyes. Then he stoops down and begins to write with his finger in the dust on the floor.*

PHARISEE   Well, what is your opinion?
Do we stone her or not?

JESUS   (*straightening up*)
Whichever one of you has never sinned should throw the first stone at her.
(*He again stoops down and continues to write in the dust. This time he writes a list of names: "Joanna — Lydda — Susanna — Marcia . . ." As each name appears, the PHARISEES begin leaving one by one without saying a word. Finally only the WOMAN remains with JESUS and the DISCIPLES. JESUS again stands erect.*)
Woman, where are the men who brought you? Has no one condemned you?

WOMAN   No one, sir.

JESUS   Neither do I. You may go.
But do not sin again.

CHORUS   *One afternoon King David took a stroll*
on the roof of his palace.
He looked down and saw a woman taking a bath.
She was extremely beautiful.
On inquiring, he learned who she was:
Bethsheba, the wife of Uriah the Hittite.
David sent for her and made love to her.
Then she went home again . . .
Later, David felt bitter remorse and prayed:
"O God, wash away my guilt,
for I have done what is wicked in Your sight."
                                    — 2 Samuel 11:1-4 / Psalm 51:2,4

SEX IS SACRED

It was high noon under the hot Italian sun.
All were drenched in sweat as they thrashed the bean pods.
18-year-old Alessandro asked to be excused for a moment.
He ran back to the farm-house for a drink.
Maria was mending a shirt while minding her baby sister.
Alessandro made his advances.
"No, Alessandro! You will go to hell! It's a sin!"
He snatched a knife from the table and struck 14 times.
"I forgive him, Lord, I forgive him. Please save his soul."
The next day Maria died in agony at the tender age of 12,
while Alessandro was sent off to prison.
50 years passed. From the balcony of St. Peter's in Rome
Pius XII declared Maria Goretti a martyr for purity.
In the square below, standing side by side,
were Maria's mother Assunta and — Alessandro.

                        ☆   ☆   ☆

Today one often hears the following complaint:
"The Church has a hang-up on sex.
Jesus was much more understanding."
Really? Let's take a look at the record:
In enumerating the 12 things that defile a person
Jesus headed the list with:
"Fornication . . . adultery . . . impurity . . ." (Mk 7:21)

Also, recall the time He reinforced the 6th commandment:
"Of old you were commanded: *Do not commit adultery.*
But I say to you:
If a man even looks at a woman with lust in his heart,
he has already committed adultery with her." (Mt 5:27-30)
He insisted that sin must be avoided at any cost:
"If your eye tempts you to sin,
tear it out and throw it away.
Better to grope your way into heaven half blind.
than to make your way clearly into the fires of hell."
Jesus stressed that God is the Author of sex:
"In the beginning He made them male and female." (Mk 10:6)
God intended sex to be used only in marriage:
"A man shall leave his parents and unite with his wife."
It's a serious sin to use sex in any other way:
masturbation: with oneself (self-abuse),
fornication: with an unmarried person,
adultery: with a married person,
homosexuality: with someone of the same sex.
"Make no mistake about it: no one still guilty of
fornication, adultery, or homosexual actions . . .
will enter the Kingdom of God." (1 Co 6:9)
Remember, three things are necessary for a sin to be MORTAL:
1. It must be something SERIOUS (stealing $100).
2. You must REALIZE it as such (not mistake it for $1).
3. You really WANT to do it (without being forced).
Thus, an action committed when one is half-asleep
can never be a serious sin,
since there is not sufficient reflection (item 2)
nor full consent of the will (item 3).
Now for some questions:
Q. "Is it wrong to read *Playboy* or see X-rated movies?"
A. Would you want to see your mother, sister, or wife
   in *Playboy's* centerfold or in that movie?
   Why not?
Q. "Is it O.K. to engage in necking and petting?"
A. It is seriously wrong for an unmarried couple.
   Sex is not a toy.
   It's not the payment for an evening's date.

It's a sacred power God has planted in our bodies
to make us co-creators with Himself.

Q. "What about french-kissing my girl?"

A. Again, it's seriously wrong. Would you allow a neighbor
to kiss your wife that way after you're married?
Why not? Because she's not his wife? Exactly!
And since she's not your wife either,
you have no right to embrace her that way now.

Q. "I'm in the habit of sinning with myself (*masturbation*).
I want to break it. What can I do"

A. First of all, go to an understanding priest
and begin with a good confession:
"Father, I need some help — I've got this problem . . ."
Try to return to the same confessor every week.
Receive Jesus in Holy Communion every Sunday.
Learn to pray the rosary every day.
Keep busy with solid companions and wholesome exercises.
Face one day at a time: "Lord, please keep me pure
not for next week, not for tomorrow, but just for today."
When tempted, repeat slowly, "Jesus, I love You."
Remember, Jesus said keeping pure is worth fighting for.
Maria Goretti proved that it's also worth dying for.

27

The Temple, a few days later. As JESUS teaches the CROWDS, a group of PHARI-SEES approaches.

Jn 8:12-56

JESUS

I am the Light of the world.
Follow me, and you will never walk in darkness.

1st
PHARISEE

You're acting as your own witness again.
Your testimony is worthless.

JESUS

The Father who sent me is also my witness.

1st
PHARISEE

Where is that father of yours?

JESUS

If you really knew me,
you would know my Father, too.
But the fact is, you know neither one of us.
If you believe what I say,
you will come to know the truth,
and the truth will set you free.

2nd
PHARISEE

Set us free? What do you mean by that?
We've never been slaves to anyone.
We're children of Abraham!

JESUS

I know that you are children of Abraham,
but you are still slaves to sin.
A slave is not a part of the family; a son is.
So if the Son sets you free,
you can be assured of your freedom.
But even as I reveal my Father to you,
you continue to do the promptings of your father.

2nd
PHARISEE

Abraham is our father!

106

JESUS	If that's the case, then do what Abraham did.
	But the fact is you are trying to kill me
	for speaking the truth that I have heard from God.
	Abraham never acted like that.
	No, you are doing what your own father does.

3rd PHARISEE	We're not illegitimate children.
	God is our only Father.

JESUS	If God were really your father, you would love me,
	since I have come from God.
	Your father is Satan, that father of lies,
	and you yearn to carry out his every wish.
	Whoever belongs to God, listens to what God says.
	The reason that you do not listen
	is that you are not His.

1st PHARISEE	You Samaritan dog! We were right after all.
	You *are* possessed by a demon!

JESUS	I am not possessed
	I seek only my Father's honor,
	while you dishonor me.
	Now listen to what I say:
	whoever is true to my word
	will never see death.

1st PHARISEE	Now we know for sure that you're possessed.
	Abraham is dead, and so are the prophets.
	Yet you say, "Whoever keeps my word will never die."
	Do you pretend to be greater than Abraham?
	Who do you think you are?

JESUS	If I were after my own glory,
	that glory would be worthless.
	It's my Father who gives me glory,
	the very one you call your God.
	But you don't even know Him.
	And if I were to say that I don't know Him,
	I would be as much a liar as you.
	Yes, I know Him and I always do what pleases Him.
	Your father Abraham was glad to see my day coming.
	He saw it and was overjoyed.

3rd	You're not even fifty yet —
PHARISEE	and you've seen Abraham?
JESUS	The absolute truth is:
	Before Abraham saw the light of day,
	I AM!

The PHARISEES *scurry in search of rocks to stone him. Exit* JESUS *with his* DISCIPLES.

☆   ☆   ☆

CHORUS   *Now Abraham and Sarah were extremely old
and Sarah was beyond the age of childbearing.
God said to Abraham: "This time next year
your wife Sarah will have a son."
Abraham burst into laughter, as he thought:
"Can a hundred-year-old man have a child?
And can Sarah bear at the age of ninety?"
God replied: "Your wife Sarah will bear you a son.
You will name him Isaac (= laughter).
With him I will establish my eternal covenant.
And in your offspring
all the nations of the earth will be blessed."*
          — Genesis 18:10,11 / 17:17-19 / 22:18

WHAT'S IN A NAME?

Moses was tending his father-in-law's sheep at Sinai.
Off in the distance he noticed a bush on fire.
"How strange! That bush keeps burning but is not destroyed.
This I have to see."
As he approached, God called to him from the bush:
"Moses, take the sandals off your feet —
you are standing on holy ground.
I am the God of your fathers, Abraham, Isaac, and Jacob.
I have heard the cry of my people in Egypt.
I now send you to Pharaoh to free them from their slavery."
Then Moses said to God:
"I shall go to the children of Israel and say to them,
'The God of your fathers has sent me to you.'
If they should ask me, 'What is His name?'

what shall I tell them?"
God said to Moses: "My name is I AM.
Tell the children of Israel: 'I AM has sent me to you.'
This shall be my name for all ages to come." (Ex 3:1-15)

☆   ☆   ☆

That's how God revealed His name (YAHWEH) to the Jews.
("Jehova" is a misspelling of YAHWEH in English.)
So great was their reverence for that name
that God's chosen people would not pronounce it.
In its place they would substitute the word "LORD" (ADONAI).
What's more, in copying the scrolls of the Old Testament,
the scribes used a special pen whenever they wrote YAHWEH!
No wonder the Jews were stunned by Jesus' statement:
"Before Abraham was born (2,000 years ago), I AM!"
He didn't say, ". . . I already existed" (= mere *pre*existence)
but rather, ". . . I AM" (= *eternal* existence).
He was using God's proper name as His own!
He was saying: "I am one with God!"

☆   ☆   ☆

Years later, St. Paul wrote of Jesus:
"God gave Him the NAME
that is greater than all other names,
so that at Jesus' NAME
every knee in all creation should bow down
and every tongue should give glory to God the Father
by proclaiming aloud:
JESUS CHRIST IS LORD (= YAHWEH)! (Phl 2:9-11)

☆   ☆   ☆

What reverence we should have for the name of Jesus!
St. Paul says that "every knee should bend . . .",
and St. Peter says that it's "the only name in all the world
that can save us." (Ac 4:12)
What a sad commentary on our society
that even "Christians" use the Holy Name irreverently!
Did you ever hear anyone in a temper swear like this:
"O Abraham!" or "For Buddha's sake!" or "Hare Krishna!"?
Then why use the name of Jesus that way?

But if you really love Him,
you will never misuse His name.
What would you do if a person said something nasty
about your best friend?
How, then, can anyone profane the name of Jesus —
without disowning Him as Lord and Master?

28 The Temple, a few days later. JESUS is seated opposite one of the trumpet-shaped money coffers with his DISCIPLES. Enter some PHARISEES.

Mk 12:1-17

PHARISEE   Rabbi, we know you teach the truth about God
regardless of what others think.
So give us your opinion on this matter:
Should we or shouldn't we pay taxes to Rome?

JESUS   Why are you trying to trap me?
Show me a tax-coin.

PHARISEE   (*fumbling in his money-bag*) Here's one.

JESUS   Whose face is that?

PHARISEE   Caesar's.

JESUS   Then give Caesar what belongs to Caesar,
and give God what belongs to God. —
Now listen to this case:
A man once planted a vineyard:
he fenced it in, dug a wine-press,
and built a tower in it.
He rented it out to tenant farmers
and then he went off on a trip.
At harvest time he sent a slave
to collect his share of grapes from the farmers.
But they attached the slave
and sent him away without a thing.
So the owner sent another slave,
who received a gash on the head.
The next one he sent was murdered;
and the others that followed
were all beaten or killed.

111

There was only one person left — his only son.*
He sent him last of all, thinking,
"Surely they will respect my son."
On seeing him, the farmers plotted together saying:
"Here comes the owner's son.
Let's kill him and the property will be ours."
So they captured him and killed him
and threw him out of the vineyard. —
Now what do you think the vineyard owner will do?

PHARISEE   Probably get rid of the tenant farmers
and rent the vineyard out to others.

JESUS   Exactly. Do you recall this scripture:
"The very stone that the builders rejected
has been used by the Lord as the cornerstone.
He has done this to our utter amazement?"

Exit JESUS *and his* DISCIPLES.

PHARISEE   What do you suppose he meant by that story?

PRIEST   Don't you recall your Isaiah?
Why, if it weren't for this fickle mob,
I'd have him arrested here and now!

☆   ☆   ☆

CHORUS   *My beloved had a vineyard on a fertile hill.*
He planted the choicest vines in it,
built a tower, and dug a wine-press.
He expected it to yield choice grapes,
but instead, it yielded only sour grapes.
The vineyard of the Lord of Hosts is Israel,
the house of Judah, His beloved vine.
He expected justice,
but instead, found only wrongdoing.
— Isaiah 5:1-7

---

* In this parable, the prophets — the greatest figures of Israel's past — when compared with Jesus ("the owner's only Son") are styled mere "slaves"!

CAESAR VERSUS GOD

He was born when England was still "Our Lady's Dowry".
When he died, England was ridding herself of "Popery".
In the 57 years that intervened,
he was husband, father, author, and diplomat;
Sheriff of London, Speaker of Parliament,
and Lord Chancellor of the entire Kingdom.
To history he is known as Sir Thomas More, Knight;
to the Church he died for, as a saint and martyr.
It all began when Henry VIII wanted a male heir.
His wife Catherine had given him a daughter
but was now barren.
Then in 1526 Henry was captivated by Anne Boleyn,
one of the maids-in-waiting on the Queen.
Anne refused to become Henry's mistress;
she would only be his queen.
Thus began the lengthy process of appealing to Pope Clement
to have the marriage with Catherine declared null and void.
Years passed. Rome procrastinated. Henry became impatient.
If the Pope would not grant Henry his divorce,
then other avenues were to be explored.
In 1530 Parliament passed a law
declaring Henry "Supreme Head of the Church in England".
All subjects were required to subscribe to this Act
or face the penalty for treason.
Thomas More refused to sign
and was taken prisoner to the Tower.
One afternoon Richard Rich paid him a visit.

Rich: "Suppose Parliament were to pass an Act
      declaring me the lawful King.
      Would not you, Master More, take me for King?"
More: "Yes, sir, that I would."
Rich: "And suppose that there were an Act of Parliament
      that all the realm should take me for Pope.
      Would not you then take me for Pope?"
More: "As to your first case, Master Rich — Parliament
      may meddle with the state of temporal princes.
      But as to the second case — suppose Parliament

would make a law that God should no longer be God.
Would you then say that God were not God?"
More's answer voiced his firm belief
that Church and State had separate spheres of authority
which were not to be confused.
"Render to Caesar the things that are Caesar's,
and to God the things that are God's." (Mk 12:17)
Several months later, he was tried;
and on the perjured testimony of Master Rich,
was found guilty of high treason against Henry.
In his defense More declared that the Oath of Supremacy
was against the laws of God and His holy Church.
He protested that no temporal prince could usurp
the supreme government of God's Church,
since it rightfully belonged "to the See of Rome,
a spiritual preeminence granted by the mouth of Our Savior,
personally present upon earth, only to St. Peter
and his successors, Bishops of the same See . . ."
Five days later, he ascended the scaffold,
declaring to the last, that he died
"the King's good servant, but God's first."

29

The Court of the Women in the Temple.
Enter a TEMPLE GUARD with ELEAZAR, a
young man. They approach a group of
PHARISEES.

Jn 9:1 to 10:16

GUARD	Here's the fellow that you wanted for questioning — the one they said was blind.
1st PHARISEE	Ah yes, young man. Tell us what happened.
ELEAZAR	The man they call Jesus made a paste of mud, smeared it on my eyes and told me: "Go and wash in the Pool of Siloam." So I went and washed, and now I can see.
1st PHARISEE	And before that, you were totally blind?
ELEAZAR	Ever since I was born.
2nd PHARISEE	But that Nazarene cannot be from God. He doesn't observe the Sabbath.
3rd PHARISEE	Yet how can a sinner give sight to the blind?
1st PHARISEE	Since you're the one he cured, young man, what is your opinion?
ELEAZAR	I think he must be a prophet.
	Enter another GUARD *with Eleazar's* PARENTS.
2nd GUARD	Rabbi, here are the boy's parents.
1st PHARISEE	Is this your son?
FATHER	Yes, that's our Eleazar.

1st *PHARISEE*	And he was born blind?
FATHER	He was.
1st *PHARISEE*	Then how do you account for his sight?
FATHER	We don't know.
1st *PHARISEE*	You don't know who opened his eyes?
MOTHER	(*impatient*) No, we don't. Ask him! He's old enough to speak for himself.
2nd *PHARISEE*	Young man, give God credit for your sight. We know that that Nazarene is a sinner.
ELEAZAR	Whether he is or not, I don't know. I only know that I was blind and now I can see.
3rd *PHARISEE*	What did he do to you? How did he cure you?
ELEAZAR	I have told you the story once. Why do you want to hear it again? Do you wish to become his disciples?
3rd *PHARISEE*	*You* are the one who's his disciple! We are disciples of Moses. We know for a fact that God spoke to Moses. But this man — we don't even know where he's from!
ELEAZAR	How strange! You don't know where he comes from, and yet he gave me my sight! We know that God does not listen to sinners, but only to those who love and respect Him. So if this man were not from God, he could not have made me see.
1st *PHARISEE*	You good-for-nothing wretch! Are you trying to teach us? Get out of here! —
	Exit ELEAZAR *with his* PARENTS. *As they leave,* *they meet* JESUS *entering with his* DISCIPLES.
JESUS	Do you believe in the Son of Man?

116

ELEAZAR	I would like to. But who is he?
JESUS	The very one speaking to you.
ELEAZAR	Yes, Lord! I do believe! (*falling to his knees*)
JESUS	I have come into this world to divide it:
	to make the blind see,
	and those who see, blind.
1st	
PHARISEE	(*overhearing*) Are you saying we are blind?
JESUS	If you were only blind, you would not be guilty.
	But you insist that you see,
	and so you continue in your guilt.
	Now listen carefully!
	Whoever gets into the sheepfold over the wall
	only wants to steal and destroy the sheep.
	It's the shepherd who comes in through the gate.
	I am the good shepherd.
	The good shepherd lays down his life for the sheep.
	A hired hand is no shepherd at all.
	For as soon as he sees a wolf coming, he runs off,
	and leaves the sheep to be torn apart and scattered.
	I am the good shepherd.
	I walk ahead of my sheep
	and they follow me because they recognize my voice.
	I lay down my life for my sheep.
	And there are other sheep I have
	that do not belong to this fold.
	I must bring them in, too.
	They will hear my voice,
	and there will be one flock
	and one shepherd.

☆   ☆   ☆

CHORUS	*The Lord is my Shepherd,*
	there is nothing that I lack.
	He leads me out to green pastures,
	and guides me beside restful waters.
	He refreshes my soul.

— *Psalm 23:1,2*

117

THE SHEEP: FED OR FLEECED?

The United States has the eagle as the national symbol;
England has the lion; and Russia, the bear.
The animal that God selected to represent His Kingdom
was the meek and helpless lamb:
"Behold the Lamb of God . . ." (Jn 1:29)
When attacked, the lamb has no wings to help it escape,
no claws, fangs, or horns to defend itself with;
not even a shell, like the turtle, in which to retreat.
Its arch-enemy, the wolf, outnumbers it six to one at birth.
How, then, does it happen that there are many more sheep
in the world today than there are wolves?
The reason is that the lamb is protected by the shepherd.
The word for shepherd in Latin is "pastor".
It comes from a verb that means "to feed",
so it really means "the feeder (of the sheep)".
Hundreds of years before Christ,
God condemned the Jewish priests,
the official leaders of His people, in the following way:
"Woe to the shepherds of Israel who feed themselves!
Should not the shepherd feed the sheep?
You drink their milk, and wear their wool,
but you do not feed the sheep.
Since they have no shepherd, my sheep are scattered,
and have become the prey of every wild beast." (Ezk 34:1-5)
Then God goes on to predict how He will right these wrongs:
"Since my shepherds are not looking after my flock,
I myself will feed my sheep:
I shall find the lost, and bring back the strays,
tend the wounded, and heal the sick.
I myself shall be a shepherd to them." (vv. 7-16)
This prediction was fulfilled in Jesus,
the good Shepherd, who became the Lamb of God,
to lay down His life on the cross for the sheep:
"Christ bore our sins in His own body on the cross.
You have gone astray like sheep, but now you have returned
to the Shepherd and *Guardian* of your souls." (1 Pt 2:24,25)
The word used for guardian in the Greek is *"episkopos"*,

the same word that gives us the word for "bishop".
Bishops are the chief shepherds of the flock of Christ.
The apostles had appointed them as their own replacements
to continue the Lord's work after they had gone.
From the start, they formed part of the Church's structure,
as is evident from the farewell speech
that St. Paul delivered to the elders of Ephesus:
"Look out for yourselves and for the entire flock
over which the Holy Spirit has made you bishops (*episkopous*)
to be shepherds of God's Church,
which He bought with His own blood.
I know that after I leave, savage wolves (false teachers)
will attack you and they will not spare the flock.
Some of these lying teachers will come from your own ranks
and try to lead the faithful astray." (Ac 20:28-30)
To avoid being led astray,
the faithful must be obedient to their pastors,
pastors must be obedient to their bishops,
bishops must be obedient to the Pope,
and the Pope must be obedient to Christ,
"the Chief Shepherd and Guardian of our souls."

30

A few minutes later, on the Temple steps, JESUS pauses a moment with his DISCIPLES.

Mt 6:16-18 / 15:12-14 / 23:27, 28 /
Lk 18:9-14

PETER   Lord, do you know that the Pharisees were shocked
by what you told them?

JESUS   Let them be.
They are blind leaders, trying to lead the blind.
And if one blind man leads another,
they will both end up in a ditch.
However, beware of their example;
for they set themselves up as models of virtue,
while all the time they are hypocrites —
just whitewashed tombs: beautiful on the outside,
but inside, full of rotting corpses.
When they fast, they parade around with sad faces
so that everyone can see them doing penance.
I tell you, they have already received their reward.
But it must not be that way with you.
When you fast, wash your face and comb your hair
so that no one suspects what you are doing.
In time your heavenly Father, who knows all secrets,
will give you your reward.
Listen carefully to this example:
Two men went up to the Temple to pray:
one was a Pharisee, and the other a tax collector.
The Pharisee stood off by himself and prayed:
"O God, I thank You that I'm not like everyone else:
thieves, liars, adulterers,
no, not even like that tax collector back there.
I fast twice a week,

120

and I give you ten percent of all that I earn."
But the tax collector stood far off,
and with head bowed, kept striking his chest
as he prayed: "O God, have mercy on me, a sinner."
I tell you, this man went home forgiven,
but not the Pharisee.
For everyone who honors himself will be humbled,
but whoever humbles himself will be honored.

☆　☆　☆

CHORUS　*God does not see as man sees;*
　　　　for man judges by outward appearances,
　　　　but the Lord looks into the heart.

— 1 Samuel 16:7

FAITH VERSUS WORKS

"The just man is saved by FAITH." (Rm 1:17)
In 1517 a German monk by the name of Martin Luther
made this his rallying cry to rebel against the Church.
He said that *faith alone* saved — *good works* were useless.
Worse still, he claimed they were invented by the Pope
to line the pockets of his priests with gold.
"All the Pharisee's good works did not save him.
The tax collector's simple trust in God's mercy did!"
He repeated the slogan:
"Sin strongly — believe more strongly."
Luther explained: "It makes no difference what you *do* —
just so you *believe* that Jesus' blood has saved you."
In translating the Bible into German, he debated
whether to include the epistle of St. James.
Why? Because James minces no words in chapter two:
"What good is it for someone to say he has faith,
if his actions do not show it?
Can that faith save him?
. . . Faith alone — without actions — is dead." (2:14-17)
Who was right and who was wrong?
Does the Church teach that we must "earn" our salvation?
Do good works deny the value of Jesus' saving death?

121

Let's examine the facts.

First, as we have already seen in section 6,
the Church has never denied the importance of faith:
"Without faith it is impossible to please God." (Heb 11:6)
But at the same time, the Church teaches
that faith must be proved by *actions*.
The Church did not invent this teaching.
She is only being faithful to what Jesus Himself taught.
Nothing is clearer from His own words.
Let us examine just one of the Gospels, *Matthew's:*

7:21 "Not everyone who *says* to me 'Lord, Lord' will be
    saved, but the one who *does* the Will of my Father."

10:42 "If anyone gives a cup of cold water to one of these
    little ones in my name, he will not lose his *reward*."

16:27 "When the Son of Man comes in glory . . . He will
    reward each one according to his *works*."

19:17 "If you wish to enter life, *keep* the commandments."

20:1-16 Jesus compares the Kingdom of Heaven (the Church)
    to a vineyard. cultivated by *workers,* who will be
    paid wages at the end of the day (= the Judgement).

23:3 "Do not follow the Pharisees example,
    for they do not *practice* what they preach."

25:14-30 Our salvation or damnation depends on how we
    have utilized our Master's money (grace) on earth.
    "You gave me five talents; I have *earned* five more."
    "Well done, good and faithful servant . . ."

25:34-46 We will be rewarded or punished to the extent
    that we *ministered* to Jesus during life.

And so we must admit
that the Lord attached great value to our actions.
Still, good works must be animated by faith.
Bishop Fulton Sheen uses a simple example
to show the interplay of faith and actions:
Good works without faith (the Pharisee's works)
are like a check made out to the amount of 000,000,0 . . .
It is worthless.
Faith in the Lord is the digit "1"
placed in front of all those zeroes: *1*,000,000,000, . . .
It gives them inestimable value.

"Joined to Me you will bear much fruit,
for without Me you can do *nothing.*" (Jn 15:5)

☆   ☆   ☆

Q. *Then isn't St. Paul contradicting Jesus in Rm 1:17?*
A. Paul is at one with the Lord's teaching.
   Luther conveniently overlooked what Paul said
   in the *very next chapter* of Romans (2:6-11):
   "He will repay each one according to his *works* . . .
   Suffering and pain to those who *do* evil,
   glory, honor, and peace to all who *do* good . . ."

31

Jn 11:1-44

JESUS

Our friend Lazarus has fallen asleep.
But I shall go and wake him.

THOMAS

Lord, if he's asleep, he must be getting better.

JESUS

Lazarus is dead.
And I am glad for your sake that I was not there because your faith will now grow stronger.

As they enter the town, MARTHA *runs to meet them.*

MARTHA

(*crying*) Lord, if you had only been here,
my brother would not have died.
But even now I know that God will do
whatever you ask Him.

JESUS

Your brother will come back to life.

MARTHA

Yes, I know, in the resurrection on the last day.

JESUS

I am the Resurrection and the Life.
Whoever believes in me
will conquer death and live.
Yes, whoever puts his faith in me here on earth
will never die.
Do you believe this, Martha?

MARTHA

Yes, Lord, I believe that you are the Son of God,
our long-awaited Messiah.

Enter MARY, *accompanied by a group of MOURNERS.*

MARY	Lord, if you had come sooner, Lazarus would still be alive.
JESUS	Where did you bury him?
MARY	Come and see. (JESUS *begins to cry.*)
1st MOURNER	(*aside*) Look, he's shedding tears. They must have been very close friends.
2nd MOURNER	Yes, but if he healed that blind man, couldn't he have kept Lazarus from dying?

ALL *walk slowly to the cave-like tomb.*

JESUS	Roll back the stone from the entrance.
MARTHA	Lord, it's already four days — There's sure to be a stench.
JESUS	Put your faith in me and you will see the glory of God!

(*Several* MOURNERS *struggle to roll back the stone.*

JESUS *raises his eyes to heaven.*)

Father, I thank you for hearing me.
I know that You always hear me.
But I spoke for the sake of the crowd,
so that they may believe that you sent me.

(*He pauses, then continues in a loud voice.*)

Lazarus, come out!

(LAZARUS *comes slowly from the tomb, bound hand and foot in the shroud.*)

Now untie him and let him go!

MOURNERS	Unbelievable! He's alive! God has visited His people!

☆   ☆   ☆

CHORUS	*The bodies of your dead will rise to life.* *You that lie in the earth, awake and rejoice!*

— Isaiah 26:19

TO LIVE FOREVER MORE

"But how can God bring a body back to life —
for example, the body of someone who's been cremated?
And even if He could, what kind of body would it be?
A young body? An old body? Or a body in its prime?"
Do these objections sound familiar?
Some people think they're being very progressive
when they say that God is powerless
to overcome all such difficulties.
Turn to First Corinthians 15:35 and you have,
almost word for word, the same objections!
In the next verse, St. Paul calls them "Stupid questions".
Then he goes on to use the example of a seed.
Outwardly, it looks deformed and dead.
Yet that seemingly lifeless seed, when planted in the ground,
gives birth to a beautiful bloom under the summer sun.
Thus, the splendor of the glorified body
will surpass that of the present mortal one,
even as the beauty of a delicate rose
is scant reminder of the seed that gave it life.
And as for the bodily resurrection itself,
we have Jesus' word that He will raise us on the last day.
Unlike the angels, we are creatures of both body and soul.
Just as our bodies worked together with our souls
for good or for evil,
so too, they will rise
to be rewarded or punished together. (Jn 5:28,29)
In the Creed we profess our faith in our immortality:
"I believe in the resurrection of the body . . ."
Benjamin Franklin summarized his Christian faith
very colorfully in the inscription he wrote for his tomb:

The Body

of

Benjamin Franklin, Printer,

(Like the cover of an old book,

Its contents torn out,

And stripped of its lettering and gilding,)

Lies here food for worms.

Yet the work itself shall not be lost,
For it will (as he believes) appear once more
In a new and beautiful Edition
Corrected and Amended
By
The Author.

32 Mid-morning, the first day of the week before Passover. In their quarters adjoining the Temple, the High Priests, ANNAS and CAIPHAS, are locked in debate.

Jn 11:45-52 / 12:9-19 / Mt 21:1-11 / 26:14-16

CAIPHAS   There is no other remedy. Lazarus must die!
Thanks to him everyone is running after that madman
— even some of our own colleagues.

ANNAS   But any violence might cause an uprising . . .

CAIPHAS   Do you hear that? (*pause*)
It sounds as if your uprising is already here.

Faint shouting in the distance. Enter two SPIES.

1st SPY   (*breathless*) My Lord Caiphas, it's all over!

CAIPHAS   Are they rioting?

1st SPY   Worse! They've declared him King!

2nd SPY   He's entering the city now, riding on a donkey . . .

1st SPY   He spent the night in Bethany with Lazarus.
Early this morning we followed him to Mount Olivet
where crowds of pilgrims from the city met him.
He mounted a donkey
and then the pilgrims began cutting palm branches
and spreading their cloaks on the road for him . . .

2nd SPY   They're calling him their king —
even the children . . .

ALL *go to the balcony. Down below there is
bedlam as the crowds milling towards the gate are
forced back by the incoming procession. Seated
calmly on a donkey,* JESUS *enters through the gate.*

129

His composure is truly royal. The CROWDS *wave palm branches and shout in unison:*

CROWDS   LONG LIVE THE KING!
BLESSED IS HE WHO COMES IN THE NAME
     OF THE LORD!
HOSANNA TO THE SON OF DAVID!

ANNAS   What are we going to do?
If we let him be, the Romans will come,
suppress our religion and destroy our nation!

CAIPHAS   You reason like an imbecile!
Why should the whole nation be destroyed for him?
Let *him* be the one to die instead of the people!

Enter a GUARD.

GUARD   Caiphas, there's someone here to see you.
He claims to be from the Galilean.

CAIPHAS   What's he doing here?
Is he armed? Did you search him?

*ALL leave the balcony and reenter the chamber.
Shortly the* GUARD *reenters with* JUDAS.

JUDAS   Peace, my lord!
I am Judas, one of Jesus' disciples.
Rumor has it that you want him arrested.

CAIPHAS   If you have come here to intimidate us . . .

JUDAS   No, No! That is not why I have come at all.
I felt perhaps I could aid you in your efforts.

CAIPHAS   In our efforts?

JUDAS   Yes. I could easily inform you
when to send your guards. — When he's alone . . .
No crowds . . . no rioting . . . You understand —

CAIPHAS   Why are you willing to do this?

JUDAS   My master is most impractical.
He does not reason as a true Israelite should,
for he has no plans to free us from Rome.
I offer suggestions. He turns a deaf ear.

130

CAIPHAS	How can you be trusted?
JUDAS	We could strike a bargain to seal the matter.
CAIPHAS	— with 30 pieces of silver?
JUDAS	Agreed, my lord!
	I shall inform you when the proper moment arrives.

☆   ☆   ☆

CHORUS	*Shout with joy, daughter of Jerusalem!*
	See, your king is coming to you:
	He comes in triumph and victory,
	but also humble and riding on a donkey.

— Zechariah 9:9

"CAN I BE SURE I'M SAVED?"

"Woe to that man by whom the Son of Man is betrayed!
Better for him if he had never been born!" (Mt 26:24)
Then why *was* he born?
Stated more broadly, the problem is this:
"Even before we draw our first breath,
God knows whether we shall be saved or lost.
Therefore, in the case of those who will be damned,
it seems as if God is partly responsible,
since He allows them to be born."
Such reasoning is faulty
for confusing "foreknowledge" with "desire".
Just because you *know* in advance that something will happen
does not mean that you *want* it to happen.
For example, imagine yourself on the roof of a skyscraper.
Looking down, you see two cars approaching at 60 MPH,
one from the west, the other from the south.
You recognize one of the cars as your father's.
You alone *know* of the collision *in advance!*
Does that mean that you *want* it to happen?
You object: "From the top of that building
I am powerless to prevent that accident.
But not so with God.
From His vantage point, He can make the sinner stop sinning."
True, He could.

131

But only at the expense of the sinner's free will.
Thus, God would be reducing the sinner to a brute animal.
However, He does not want *robots* who are forced into action.
He wants *children* who will love and serve Him freely.
"Let us make man in our own image and likeness." (Gn 1:26)
When God blessed man with free will,
He opened the door to the possibility
that some men might misuse that gift
by choosing the creature in place of the Creator.
Still, "God does not want the death of the sinner,
rather He wants him to be converted and live." (Ezk 33:11)

☆　　☆　　☆

The tragic case of Judas disproves what is held
by the followers of Calvin and Knox.
These men taught:
"Once you accept Jesus as your personal Lord and Savior,
it is impossible to be lost."
Their view contradicts the teaching of Scripture:
Ezk 33:12 "When a good man chooses to sin,
　　　　　　his former goodness will not save him."
1 Co 9:27 "But I control my body and subdue it,
　　　　　　so that I, having preached to others,
　　　　　　may not be lost myself."
Phl 2:12 "Work at your salvation in fear and trembling."
Why so, if you are *assured* of your salvation
simply by accepting Jesus as Lord and Savior?
Finally, if it is impossible to reject the Lord
once you have accepted Him, why bother praying,
"Lead us not into temptation"?

33

Late the next afternoon. JESUS and the TWELVE have climbed the Mount of Olives, facing the Temple buildings across the Kedron valley.

Mk 13:1-37 / Lk 17:28-30; 21:20-24 / Mt 25:31-46

JAMES   What magnificent buildings! They'll last fovever!

JESUS   Not so! For I tell you the day is coming
when every single stone will be thrown down.

The DISCIPLES look at one another in amazement.

PETER   Tell us, Lord, when will that happen?

JESUS   When you see the hated pagen idol
set up in the Holy of Holies —
just as the prophet Daniel predicted —
then you must escape from the City.
And when you see Jerusalem surrounded by troops,
know for certain she will soon be destroyed.
Then the ones in Judea must escape to the mountains;
for those days will be days of doom,
when all that Scripture says will be fulfilled.
But how tragic those days will be
for nursing and expectant mothers!
The wrath of God will descend on this chosen race:
many will fall by the sword;
the rest will be led away captive to every nation.
And Jerusalem will be occupied by the Gentiles
until that day when nations are united.
The horror of those days has not been seen on earth
since God created the world;
and will not be seen again,
until the final day of destruction.

133

ANDREW	And when will that take place?
JESUS	First, this Gospel must be preached

JESUS First, this Gospel must be preached
throughout the entire world.
Yet even with that,
sin will become so widespread
that the love of many will grow cold.
It will be as it was in the days of Lot;
everyone steeped in pleasures and worldly cares.
But on the day that Lot left Sodom
it rained fire and brimstone from heaven
and killed them all.
That is how it will be on the Day of my return.
That day will be preceded by terrifying events:
nations and kingdoms locked in mortal combat;
earthquakes, famines, and epidemics everywhere.
In the heavens, strange signs will appear
in the sun, the moon, and the stars.
On earth men will shake with terror
at the raging seas and tidal waves.
Then my sign will appear in the sky,
and all the peoples of the earth will tremble
as they look up and see me, the Son of Man,
coming with glory on the clouds of heaven.
I shall send my angels with a mighty trumpet-blast
to gather all peoples from the ends of the earth.
As I sit on my throne of glory,
all mankind will assemble before me.
I shall separate them as a shepherd does his flock:
the sheep on my right, the goats on my left.
Then I shall say to the ones on my right:
"Come, my Father's chosen ones,
come and take possession of the Kingdom
that has been waiting for you since time began.
For in my hunger you gave me food,
and in my thirst you gave me drink.
I had no clothes and you supplied them.
I was homeless and you took me in.
I was sick and in prison and you came to visit me."
Then they will ask:

"Lord, when did we ever give you any food?
Or quench your thirst?
Or supply you with clothing?
When did we see you homeless and take you in?
And when were you ever sick or in prison
for us to visit you?"
And I will answer them:
"Whatever you did for any of my brothers,
you were really doing for me."
Then I will say to those on my left:
"Away from me, you cursed ones!
Away to the unquenchable fire
that was prepared for Satan and his angels.
For in my hunger and thirst you ignored me.
When I was cold and away from home,
you turned your back on me.
I was sick and in prison but you did not visit me."
Then they, too, will ask:
"Lord, when did we ever see you in need
and fail to help you?"
And I will answer:
"Whenever you refused to help any of my brothers,
you were refusing to help me."
They will be condemned to eternal punishment,
while my chosen ones will enter eternal life.

☆　　☆　　☆

CHORUS　　*In those days the archangel Michael will appear.*
Then there will be a period of suffering
never before seen on the face of the earth.
Those asleep in their graves will awake:
Some to everlasting life, others to eternal doom.
　　　　　　　　　　　　　　　　　— Daniel 12:1,2

THE COMMUNION OF SAINTS

He was on his way to ferret out more Christians
— all doomed to die —
when he was thrown to the ground by a flash of light.
A Voice cried out: "Saul, Saul, why are you persecuting me?"

"Who are you, Lord?", he asked.
"I am Jesus, the one you are persecuting." (Ac 9:1-5)
Thus, Christianity's arch-enemy became her chief witness:
Saul the bigot became Paul the Apostle.
Right from his first encounter with the Lord
St. Paul was confronted with the beautiful reality
of the Mystical Body of Christ.
As he groveled in the dust, he may have thought:
"But, Jesus, I'm not persecuting *you;*
I'm only going after those *Christians.*"
The Lord had solved that difficulty years before:
"Whatever you do to the least of *my brothers,*
that you do unto *Me.*" (Mt 25:40)
Jesus identifies Himself with all those who believe in Him.
This truth we call the *Mystical Body* of Christ.
St. Paul would elaborate on it many times in his letters:
Col 1:18 "Christ is the Head of the Church,
   which forms His body."
Rm 12:4,5 "Just as it takes many parts to form one body,
   — and each part has its own separate function —
   in the same way, we all form one body in Christ:
   we are joined to each other as parts of the same body."
Did you know that you profess belief in the Mystical Body
every time you recite the words of the Creed:
"I believe in the Communion of saints"?
That means we are *united with* all the faithful:
1) *on earth:* the Church Militant (still fighting to be saved)
2) *in purgatory:* Church Suffering (still being purified)
3) *in heaven:* Church Triumphant (already in glory).
Like the countless cells in a body —
with each individual cell depending on the others
to help sustain its own life —
we members of Christ's Body can help one another
through intercessory prayer.
"There should be no divisions within the body:
each part should be concerned for all the other parts.
If one part feels pain, the other parts feel it, too;
and if one part is honored, the other parts share the joy."
                                        (1 Co 12:25,26)

136

34

Sunset, three days later. A large, upper room on the west side of Jerusalem. JESUS and his DISCIPLES enter and begin reclining on the dining couches around a U-shaped table.

Jn 13 / Lk 22:14-27 / Mt 26:26-29

PETER   James, that place was meant for me!

JAMES   You're mistaken, Simon!
My brother and I belong on the right and left.

JESUS   Rulers here on earth like to make their power felt.
But it should never be that way with you.
In your case, the one who is the greatest
should be ready to serve the rest.

*PETER goes sulking to the lowest couch. JESUS
crosses to the side, removes his robe, wraps
a towel around his waist, fills a basin with
water, and then proceeds to wash the feet of
each DISCIPLE. He comes to PETER.*

PETER   Lord, are you going to wash *my* feet?

JESUS   At this time, you don't understand what I am doing;
later on, you will see it clearly.

PETER   O no! I will *never* let you wash my feet.

JESUS   If I don't wash you,
you shall be cut off from me.

PETER   In that case, Lord, then wash not just my feet,
but the rest of me, as well.

*JESUS completes the washing, returns the basin to
the side, dons his robe, and then reclines at table.*

137

JESUS	Do you realize what I have done for you?
	You call me your Lord and Master, and I am.
	Yet I have performed the chore of a slave!
	In this, I have given you an example to follow. —
	Now let us begin this meal,
	which I have long desired to eat with you
	before I suffer.

JOHN *(asking the ritual question from Exodus 12:26)*
"Lord, what is the meaning of this ritual?"

JESUS "It is the Passover of the Lord.
For He passed over the houses of the Israelites
in Egypt. He struck down the first-born
of the Egyptians; but our houses He spared."

*(They continue with the ritual meal, until the
third cup of benediction. JESUS takes one of
the flat loaves of unleavened bread in his hands,
looks up to heaven, blesses and breaks it.)*

Take this and eat it:
This is my body.

*(The DISCIPLES each take a piece and consume it.
JESUS takes a cup of wine and blesses it.)*

Drink this, all of you:
For this is my blood of the new covenant.
It will be shed to wash away the sins of all.
You are to repeat this action
as a reminder of my death.

*(The cup is passed around and ALL drink from it.
JESUS appears deeply troubled.)*

Listen, all of you:
One of you is about to betray me.

A moment of stunned silence, followed by murmuring.

DISCIPLES *(to each other)* Is he serious?
Who could it be?

PETER *nods to* JOHN *to find out who it is.*

JOHN *(leaning back on JESUS' chest)* Who is it, Lord?

138

JESUS	The one to whom I give this bread.
	(*He takes a morsel of bread, dips it in bitter sauce and hands it to* JUDAS *on the far couch, saying quietly:*) Now, go and do what you must.
	JUDAS *exits quickly.*
THOMAS	Where is he going? — To buy more supplies?
PHILIP	Either that — or to give something to the poor.
JESUS	Now my hour of glory is fast approaching. And my Father will be glorified in me. I will not be with you much longer, yet none of you can come with me now.
PETER	Lord, why can we not go with you? I am ready to die for you!
JESUS	You are ready to die for me, Simon? Listen carefully: This very day, before cockcrow, you will deny me three times.
PETER	Never! I would sooner die!
JESUS	As I leave you, I give you a new commandment: love one another as I have loved you. Your love for one another will be a sign to all the world that you are my disciples. Come, let us go from here. (ALL *exit.*)

☆　　☆　　☆

CHORUS	*Moses built an altar with twelve stones, representing the twelve tribes of Israel. Then he sprinkled the people with the blood of the sacrifice and said: "This is the blood of the Covenant which the Lord has made with you."*

— Exodus 24:4,8

MEMORIAL DAY: A PARABLE

Years ago there was a boy who had a favorite older brother.
They were inseparable — until the war forced them apart.
From the front, the older brother often wrote,
telling his kid-brother, how fond of him he was
and how proud he was to be defending him.
The younger brother saved each letter in a special drawer,
to be reread from time to time with admiration.
He longed to see the day when his brother would return.
Then, one gloomy Friday — a telegram arrived.
"Official. From the War Department."
Through tear-filled eyes, his mother read the words:
". . . killed in action."
Memorial Day arrived and brought a visitor in uniform.
With parcel underarm, he came to see our grieving friend.
"I was your brother's buddy in the same platoon.
I was with him when he died.
I thought you'd like to see the uniform he wore
as a reminder of his courage.
Look there — it's stained with his own blood."

☆   ☆   ☆

"How improbable!" you say?
Well, it really happened.
You see, we Christians are that younger brother.
The human race — our country — was at war with Sin,
a war that we had lost —
until God's only Son became our Older Brother.
He donned our uniform of fragile flesh.
and went to sacrifice Himself for us.
We have the letters that He wrote as God's inspired Word.
We hear them read again at the first part of the Mass.
Then comes the solemn moment of the Great Memorial,
when the priest — fellow-soldier of our Blessed Lord,
holds high the uniform He wore the day He died:
"This is my body — now given for you."
"This is my blood — poured out for all."
Thus, time and space give way to that eternal moment
when He shed His blood for us on Calvary:

140

"When we eat this Bread and drink this Cup,
we proclaim Your death, Lord Jesus,
until You come in glory." (1 Co 11:26)
In doing so, we share the promise that He made
that afternoon in Galilee:
"The bread that I shall give will be my flesh." (Jn 6:51)
He is really present on our altars:
not as symbol, not as sign,
but as Himself: Body and Blood, Soul and Divinity.
You ask: "How can that be? And why?"
The *"how"* we leave to God's almighty power.
The *"why"* was given when He showed His love for us:
"No one has a greater love than this:
to give his *life* for those he loves." (Jn 15:13)
"Whoever eats my flesh and drinks my blood
has eternal life,
and I will raise him up on the last day." (Jn 6:54)

35

The Mount of Olives, an hour later. JESUS is about to enter the olive grove with the ELEVEN.

Mt 26:36-56 / Jn 18:1-11 / Lk 22:43,44

JESUS

Simon, James, John — come with me.
The rest wait here, while I go to pray.

(*The* EIGHT DISCIPLES *sit down near the entrance, while* JESUS *enters the grove with the* THREE DISCIPLES.)

My soul is almost crushed to death with sorrow.
Wait here and keep watch with me.

(*The* THREE *sit down, while* JESUS *goes on about a stone's throw. He falls to the ground.*)

Father, — if it is possible,
take this bitter cup of suffering from me —
but only if it be Your will.

(*He lies prostrate on the ground. Long moments pass. He stands and returns to the* THREE.)

Simon, are you asleep?
You could not stay awake for just one hour?
Stay awake and pray, to overcome all temptation.
The spirit is willing, but the flesh is weak.

(JESUS *returns to his former position.*)

Father — my Father, if I must drink of this cup,
then Your holy Will be done!

(*Suddenly, the earth seems to split open.* JESUS *sees an immense* ARMY OF SOULS *marching down the corridors of time. As they pass him, column by column, they give their death-rattle chant.*)

143

1st *GROUP*	A curse on all the poor in spirit — May greedy thieves and misers prosper, and all exploiters of the poor . . .
2nd *GROUP*	A curse on all of those who weep — Blessed be all drunkards, gamblers, all peddlers of drugs and acid rock . . .
3rd *GROUP*	A curse on all the meek and lowly — Praised be arrogance and pride, and bitter hatred towards all parents . . .
4th *GROUP*	A curse on those who thirst for justice — Up with liars, perjurors, all willful heretics . . .
5th *GROUP*	A curse on those who show compassion — May all murderers and racists prosper . . .
6th *GROUP*	A curse on all the pure of heart — Long live adultery, impurity, and sodomy and every type of base pornography . . .
7th *GROUP*	Away with all the peacemakers — May unjust wars and quarrels never cease . . .
8th *GROUP*	A curse on all the little children, for they were only meant for heaven — Long live all doctors, nurses, and women who abort!

Finally, a dark SHADOW *approaches* JESUS.

SATAN	Why go on? For all of these it's just as if you never came or lived or died.
JESUS	(*with blood pouring from his sweat glands*) Father, — not my will, but Yours be done! (*An* ANGEL *appears and comforts* JESUS. *He struggles to his feet and returns to the* THREE.) Are you still sleeping? Wake up! It is time to go. My betrayer is here. (*Suddenly enter* JUDAS, *leading a band of* TEMPLE GUARDS, *all with torches and clubs.* JESUS *goes forward to meet them.*) Who is it you are looking for?

A GUARD	Jesus of Nazareth!
JESUS	I am the one. (*They fall back, petrified.*)
JUDAS	(*approaches and kisses* JESUS) Good evening, Rabbi!
JESUS	Judas, do you betray me with a kiss?
MALCHUS	(*seizing* JESUS) The rope, quick!
PETER	Lord, should we attack now? (*Draws a sword and strikes* MALCHUS *on the right ear.*)
JESUS	Simon, put away your sword. Don't you know that I could ask the Father for more than 12,000 angels to defend me? But then, how could I drain the cup which He has given me?
	(*The* GUARDS *bind* JESUS *with a rope.*)
	Am I a criminal that you had to come with swords and clubs to take me? While I was teaching in the Temple every day, you never laid a hand on me. No — you wait for darkness to do your work.
	DISCIPLES *run off.* GUARDS *lead* JESUS *away captive.* PETER *and* JOHN *follow at a distance.*
CHORUS	*I looked for sympathy, but there was none;* *for someone to comfort me, but I found no one.* — *Psalm 69:20*

TRANSFIGURED / DISFIGURED

His approaching passion filled Jesus with dread:
"My soul is sorrowful to the point of death." (Mk 14:34)
The chosen three — Peter, James, and John —
had been invited to comfort Him — but they slept!
Six months earlier, Jesus had taken the same three disciples
up a very high mountain and was *transfigured* before them:
"His face shone like the sun,
and His clothes became as white as snow." (Mt 17:2)
For one fleeting moment, His divinity broke through
the frail trapping of His humanity —

a sight which caused Peter to exclaim:
"Lord, it is good for us to be here!" (Mt 17:4)
On Olivet, He sweat blood — while his disciples slept.
On Thabor, He shone like the sun — and overawed them.
Such contrasts coexisting in the same Person!
What is the explanation?
Here we are dealing with the HYPOSTATIC UNION,
that is, the union of two natures in one Person.
To understand this union more properly,
we must first clarify our terms.
If you asked someone, "Who just called you on the phone?",
and received the answer, "A human being",
you would rightly take that as a curt reply.
For you requested the name of a *person* (= "who")
but the answer you received was a *nature* (= "what").
(It's self-evident that only human beings use phones.
It's beyond the *nature* of an animal or an angel to do so.)
Therefore, we can define "person" and "nature" as follows:
person: an individual who can know and love ("Who?")
nature: the inner force of action or behavior ("What?")
Simply stated, then, the hypostatic union means:
Jesus is only *one* person: a *divine* Person (God the Son)
with *two* natures:

    1) *divine,* which He shares with Father and Holy Spirit,
    2) *human,* which He received in Mary's womb.

Furthermore, these natures are so joined in the one Person,
that each nature retains its *own distinct properties.*
There is no "fusion" of the two natures!
(To illustrate:
When *salt is mixed with* water,
each retains its own properties in the resulting solution.
By contrast, when *hydrogen* joins with *oxygen* to form water,
both lose their original properties of combustibility, etc.)
We can summarize all that has been said as follows:

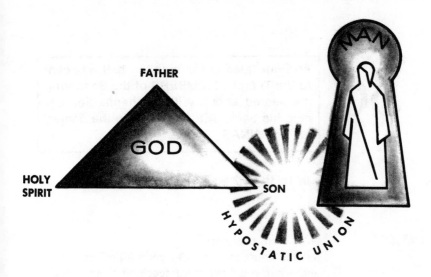

Jesus, the eternal Son of God, is true GOD and true MAN:

as GOD:	as MAN:
"begotten of the Father before all ages . . ."	"in the fullness of time, was born of a woman . . ."
	Ga 4:4
"begotten, not made . . ."	". . . was made flesh"
	Jn 1:14
"His nature was divine . . ."	"took on the nature of a slave . . ."
	Phl 2:6
"God from God . . ."	". . . one mediator, the man Jesus Christ . . ."
	1 Tm 2:5
is all-knowing	"grew in (human) wisdom"
	Lk 2:52
quelled the storm	slept during the storm
	Mk 4:38
was David's Lord	was David's offspring
	Mt 22:45
shared the Father's will: "I and the Father are one."	had a human will: "Your Will, not mine be done."
Jn 10:30	*Mk 14:36*
transfigured on Mt. Thabor	disfigured on Mt. Olivet
Is the eternal "I AM"	"He bowed his head and died."
Jn 8:58	*Jn 19:30*

147

36

An hour later in the meeting hall adjacent to the Temple. MEMBERS of the Sanhedrin are seated about. With his hands tied behind his back, JESUS stands in the center, facing ANNAS.

Jn 18:19-24 / Mk 14:55-65 / Lk 22:67-71

ANNAS
Now then, prisoner,
tell the court exactly who your followers are,
and what you have been teaching them.

JESUS
I have held no secret meetings.
I have always taught in public —
both in the synagogues and in the Temple.
Why question *me* about my teaching?
Ask the ones who heard me. They know what I
said.

GUARD
(*slapping* JESUS *across the mouth*)
Is that any way to answer the High Priest?

JESUS
If what I said is a lie,
use it as evidence against me.
But if it's the truth, then why did you strike me?

Enter CAIPHAS *and other* MEMBERS *of the
Sanhedrin.*

ANNAS
Ah Caiphas!
I was doing some preliminary questioning.
But the prisoner has been most uncooperative.

CAIPHAS
Is he aware how serious the charges are?
(*to* JESUS) Nazarene, they could mean your *life*.
(*glancing about*) I now call this court to order.
Prosecutor, summon the first witness.

PROSECUTOR	Levi, the scribe, take the stand, please.
	(LEVI *rises and moves slowly out to center.*)
	Do you recognize the prisoner?
LEVI	I do. He's Jesus from Nazareth.
PROSECUTOR	Please tell the court what you know about him.
LEVI	Well, last year during the feast of Purim, he told old Ben-Judah at the pool of Bethsaida to carry his sleeping-mat away. But it happened to be the Sabbath.
PROSECUTOR	You mean the prisoner ordered him to violate God's holy law of the Sabbath rest?
LEVI	That he did.
NICODEMUS	(*from the side, rising*) I object! He was curing a man of his paralysis. He had no intention of breaking the Sabbath.
ANNAS	Objection overruled! He has broken the Sabbath repeatedly! Why, on one occasion he even called himself the lord of the Sabbath!
	Loud discussion in the hall.
CAIPHAS	(*enfuriated*) SILENCE! (*then calmly*) Prisoner, what is your answer to these charges? (*pause*) We are still waiting. (*longer pause*) Very well, prosecutor, summon the next witness.
PROSECUTOR	Joel Bar-Simeon, to the stand. (JOEL *obliges.*) Now then, tell us what you know about the prisoner.
JOEL	This time two years ago, the accused took a whip and mercilessly drove the merchants from the Temple. When we demanded some explanation, he answered: "I will destroy this man-made Temple, and in three days I will build another, that is not made by human hands."

149

Shocked murmuring around the hall.

CAIPHAS Well, prisoner —
what have you to say in your defense? (*pause*)
Still no answer? In that case, (*He rises.*)
I order you in the name of the living God
to tell us if you are our long-awaited Messiah!

JESUS I am.
And some day you shall see me
sitting on the Father's right
and coming on the clouds of heaven!

Gasps of horror around the hall.

CAIPHAS (*very deliberately*) Nazarene,
are you implying that the Almighty is your father?

JESUS I am His one and only Son.

CAIPHAS (*tearing his robe from neck to waist in a rage*)
Why waste *time* on more witnesses?
You have heard the *blasphemy* for yourselves.
Members of the Sanhedrin, what is your verdict?

ALL (*shouting together*) Death!
He is guilty of death!
Give him death!

*ALL surround JESUS and begin to beat on him,
shouting, "Blasphemer! Liar! Imposter!"*

PROSECUTOR Gentlemen, please! (*continues with sarcasm*)
This is now way to treat so illustrious a prisoner
as God's own son. After all —

(*He blindfolds JESUS and motions to a bystander
to strike his cheek; he continues with contempt.*)

All right, you prophet. Suppose you tell us.
Who was it that struck you?

Peals of laughter. The banter continues.

☆   ☆   ☆

CHORUS *He was treated cruelly, but took it humbly;
he did not say a word.*

150

Like a lamb led off to be slaughtered,
like a sheep that is mute during shearing,
he did not say a word.
He was taken by force and sentenced;
not a soul showed concern for his fate.
— Isaiah 53:7,8

LIAR, LUNATIC, OR LORD?

The thinking of many people goes something like this:
"Jesus was a good man — a great moral leader,
but don't ask me to believe he was God."
O.K. Suppose an imposter tries to con you. Any opinion?
"He'd be a two-faced swindler."
Suppose someone else tries to tell you he's Julius Caesar.
"He ought to see a shrink — fast!"
Well, if Jesus isn't God,
He belongs in one of those two categories.
But He cannot be "just a great moral leader."
You see, a great moral leader would never claim to be God
unless, of course, — he really was!
Yet Jesus made that claim many times: scenes 7, 16, 27, 30.
At His trial, however, He leaves no room for doubt:
His judges want Him executed. (Mk 14:55)
Their witnesses fail to supply a capital offense.
Jesus takes the stand and is put under oath.
He must tell the truth or perjure Himself.
"Are you the Messiah we've been waiting for?"
He replies, "I am." (still no capital offense)
and continues: "Someday, you shall see me return:
1) *sitting at God's right hand*
   The right is the place of honor.
   It is reserved only for equals or superiors.
   So Jesus is saying: "I am God's equal."
2) *and coming on the clouds of heaven."*
   In the O.T. *clouds* are a sign of God's presence:
   Ex 19:9 God said, "I will come to you in a thick cloud."
   Ps 104:3 "Lord, You use the clouds as Your chariot."
At this, the High Priest tears his robes.

151

That was something Jews did only when:
1) a close relative or friend died (2 Sm 1:11) or
2) someone claimed a prerogative that was God's. (2 Kg 5:7)
The punishment for this was death. (Lv 24:16)
Before Pilate, the Jewish leaders admitted as much:
"We have a law that says he must die
for claiming to be the Son of God." (Jn 19:7)
So there you have it.
As C. S. Lewis put it:
"You must make your choice.
Either this man was, and is, the Son of God:
or else a madman
or something worse.
You can shut Him up for a fool,
you can spit at Him and kill Him as a demon;
or you can fall at His feet and call Him Lord and God.
But let us not come with any patronizing nonsense
about His being a great human teacher.
He has not left that open to us.
He did not intend to."

— *Mere Christianity* (Macmillan, N.Y. 1943) p. 56

37

Minutes later in the courtyard of the Priests' residence. Around an open fire stands a group of GUARDS and SERVANTS. Lost in the group stands PETER. Enter a SCRIBE on the balcony.

Jn 18:15-18, 25-27 / Lk 22:54-62

SCRIBE
Praise God! He's convicted!
The verdict is death!

1st
GUARD
On what grounds?

SCRIBE
(*descending stairs*) Blasphemy!
He made himself one with God!

2nd
GUARD
He sounds more like a lunatic.

SCRIBE
All the same, he must die.
The Law decrees the stoning of anyone
who claims to be divine. —
He'll be hanging from a cross by sundown !

PETER
But you just said that the penalty was stoning.

SCRIBE
It is — but he deserves to die like a criminal.
At dawn, we turn him over to the Romans. —
Why should you be concerned, anyway?

HOUSE-
MAID
I know why! — He's one of his followers.
I let him in the gate an hour ago.
But he denied having anything to do with him.

PETER
That's right, woman. I don't know the man!

2nd
GUARD
Are you sure? (*moving in on* PETER)
Why, even that accent of yours gives you away.

153

PETER	I repeat: I don't know the man! I swear it!
	(*moves nervously to the far end of the courtyard*)
3rd GUARD	Wait! I recognize you now! I saw you in the garden when we arrested him. You cut off my cousin's ear.
PETER	(*turning on him*) May I burn in hell if I'm acquainted with that imposter! So get away from me — (*Suddenly a rooster crows. PETER looks up to see JESUS being led across the upper balcony. JESUS' battered face looks down on him with pity. PETER murmurs as he stumbles away:* O Lord, what have I done? — What have I done? — (*breaks out sobbing*) Forgive me — please, forgive me — (*Exits, crying bitterly.*)

☆   ☆   ☆

CHORUS *If an enemy had done this,*
I could have endured it.
But it was you, my trusted companion and friend,
after we had walked and spoken together
in the House of God.

— Psalms 55:12-15

WHAT ABOUT THE BAD POPES?

He was tense as he sat across from me.
He grew even more tense as he reviewed the sordid facts.
"Do you expect me to believe
that a church headed by
an Alexander VI with his illegitimate children,
a Julius II with his plundering army,
and the rest of those Renaissance Popes,
is really the true Church founded by Jesus Himself?
It sounds more like the church of the anti-Christ!"
I asked him if he accepted the Old Testament as God's word.
"Every last verse of it."
"Do you believe that God chose the Jews as His own people?"
"Absolutely."

"And that the Bible tells the truth about them?"
"Of course I do."
"Thank you", I concluded. "You have just reinforced my faith
that the Catholic Church is God's only true Church."
His bewildered expression searched for some explanation.
"You see, if there is one undeniable fact
that leaps out from countless chapters of the Old Testament,
it is this:
the obstinacy and disloyalty of God's Chosen People,
and especially of the leaders of His People.
Let's start with Saul: gross disobedience to God (1 Sm 15:11),
David: adultery followed by murder (2 Sm 11),
Solomon: idolatry and innumerable infidelities (1 Kg 11).
In 2nd Kings every other chapter contains the refrain:
"Like his father, he sinned against the Lord . . ." (2 Kg 21:20)
Yet in spite of it all, they were still God's Chosen People.
What's more, if the very first Pope —
who had been handpicked by Jesus Himself —
cursed and swore that he did not know his Master,
it doesn't surprise me that in the course of 2,000 years
there have been some others who have done the same.
No, the really surprising thing is
that in spite of many weak and even sinful Popes,
the Church has survived —
and not merely survived, but even flourished —
still teaching with the same authority that Jesus gave her.
Do not confuse sinlessness with infallibility.
Alexander VI may have been immoral
but he never legalized his immorality with a papal decree.
A moment ago, you called the Pope "anti-Christ".
Well, if they called the Head of the house "Beelzebul",
it doesn't upset me that those of His own household
have been defamed as anti-Christs and demons. (Mt 10:25)
In examining this emotionally-charged issue of the papacy,
it would be well to recall the sound advice of Gameliel
concerning the behavior of Peter and his flock:
'If this work is of human origin, it is bound to fail.
But if it is of God, you will not be able to destroy it —
indeed, you may find yourselves at war with God.' " (Ac 5:39)

I had finished.
My visitor had turned pale.
He took his coat, said good-night, and left at once.

☆ ☆ ☆

On a more practical level,
we can learn a very powerful lesson from Peter's denials:
Avoid occasions of sin like the plague!
Remember, if David with all his meekness,
if Solomon, with all his wisdom,
if Peter with all his determination —
if these men, so favored by God, failed and sinned —
then at the first sign of temptation
the surest weapon is
prayer and escape!

38

Sunrise, two hours later. The PRIESTS and GUARDS stand with JESUS in the court-yard of the Roman Governor's residence. Enter ATTENDANT.

Jn 18:28-38 / Lk 23:1-7

ATTENDANT   The governor will see you now.

ANNAS   Our Law forbids us to enter a gentile's home today.

We must remain ritually clean for the Passover.

(*Exit* ATTENDANT. *In a moment, enter* PILATE.)

PILATE   (*bruskly*) Just what is it that you want?

ANNAS   A sentence of death for this prisoner!

PILATE   What are the charges?

ANNAS   If he were not a criminal, your honor, we would not have troubled you in the first place.

PILATE   In that case, *you* pass sentence on him — within the limits of your own law. (*turns to exit*)

ANNAS   But we lack authority to enforce the death penalty. And as for charges, he is a rabble-rouser, he forbids us to pay taxes to Caesar, and he claims to be our king!

PILATE   A king? — (*motions to* SOLDIER *to lead* JESUS *inside. They exit.* PILATE *seats himself.*) Is it true? Are you their king?

JESUS   Do you ask this from your own investigations or from what you just heard?

PILATE   (*angered*) I am no Jew, am I? Your own leaders had you arrested, not I! (*calmly*) Now then, what have you done?

157

JESUS	My kingdom does not belong to this world. If it did, my followers would have fought to have kept me from being arrested. But my kingdom is elsewhere.
PILATE	So you *are* a king!
JESUS	Yes, I am a king. The reason I was born, the very reason I came into the world is to witness to the truth. All who stand for truth, welcome my voice.
PILATE	Truth? (*sneering*) What on earth is that? (*exits to balcony and addresses* JEWISH LEADERS *below.*) I have just examined the prisoner, and I find him not guilty.
ANNAS	But he causes riots wherever he goes — from here all the way to his native Galilee!
PILATE	Is he from Galilee?
SCRIBE	Yes! From the town of Nazareth.
PILATE	Then he's in Herod's jurisdiction. How fortunate! Herod is in town for the festival. Let *him* make the decision. Take the prisoner away.

☆ ☆ ☆

CHORUS	*The Lord said to David:* *"When you die and are resting with your ancestors, I will place one of your offspring on your throne. I will establish his kingdom forever. I will be a father to him — and he will be a son to me."*

— 2 Samuel 7:12-14

"THY KINGDOM COME"

At His birth, Magi came from the East in search of
"the one who is born King of the Jews." (Mt 2:2)
To Pilate, Jesus admitted that He was a King —

but not a rival of Caesar or Herod:
"My kingdom is not of this world." (Jn 18:36)
Jesus came to establish a spiritual kingdom.
Did He ever describe it?
Yes, whenever He spoke of the "Kingdom of Heaven".
The word "heaven" in that phrase misleads many into thinking
that Jesus' kingdom has nothing to do with the present life.
They fail to realize that pious Jews usually substituted
the word "heaven" for "God" out of respect.
Even today, we do the same thing in such phrases as
"for heaven's sake" and "Heaven forbid!"
(Matthew, who wrote for the Jews, has "heaven"
where Mark and Luke use the word "God".)
So "Kingdom of *Heaven*" simply means "Kingdom of *God*".
Though it looks forward to the future life,
God's kingdom has already begun here on earth.
If you want to prove that Jesus' Kingdom —
while spiritual — has its roots planted in this world,
read the parables of the Kingdom in Matthew 13.

The parable of the Weeds and the Wheat is the clearest:

PARABLE (vv. 24-30)	ITS MEANING (vv. 36-43)
The sower	Jesus (the Son of Man)
plants good seed	converts people to the Kingdom
in his field.	in the world.
An enemy plants weeds.	Satan converts the wicked.
Workers want weeds uprooted.	Disciples want evildoers out.
The master intervenes:	Jesus decides:
"Let them grow side by side	"Let them live together
until the harvest.	until Judgement Day.
I will send the harvesters	I will send my angels
to pull up the weeds first	to separate all evildoers
and burn them.	and throw them into hell.
Put the wheat into my barn."	The just will go to heaven."

Jesus prefaced this parable by saying:
"The kingdom of *heaven* is like this." (v. 24)
Yet what follows refers to life on *earth:*

159

saints and sinners living side by side until the Last Day.
Therefore, the kingdom of heaven begins here on earth.
Another word for that kingdom is "the *Church*".
Recall the passage in Mt 16, where Jesus says
in v. 18: "on this rock I will build my *Church*"
in v. 19: "the keys of the *kingdom of heaven*".
According to the rules of Hebrew parallelism,
these two expressions are synonymous.
Furthermore, the other parables in Mt 13 bear this out:
like a *mustard seed,* the Church has small beginnings;
like *yeast* in flour, she will spread through the world;
as seed is planted in *different types of soil,*
so too, some of her members fall away at once,
others are stifled by worldly cares and pleasures,
and others persevere to give an abundant yield,
"While she slowly grows to maturity,
the Church longs for the completed kingdom,
and with all her strength, she hopes and desires
to be united in glory with her King."

(Vatican II, Lumen Gentium, 5)

39 Herod's court, an hour later. JESUS stands bound, surrounded by the PRIESTS and GUARDS. Enter HEROD, half-drunk from the previous night's orgy.

Lk 23:8-12

HEROD   What a rare pleasure! We meet at last!
          I have heard that you perform miracles, Nazarene.
          (*seating himself*) Tell us, what is your secret?
          (*pause. Continues in paternalistic tone.*)
          Come now, don't be shy. You're among friends.
          (*laughter, followed by more silence*) I see —
          perhaps you would like some subject to work with?
          Very well! (*snaps his fingers*) Jester! Over here!
          (*Enter JESTER. His nose is grotesque.*) Now then,
          suppose you take two inches off my jester's nose.
          laughter; pause) Come, magician, we are waiting!

ANNAS   Your Highness, this is no joking matter.
          This man is a blasphemer.
          Pilate has turned him over to you for sentencing.
          The situation is most serious!

JESTER   Serious? And what make you think
          that two inches off my nose is not serious?
          (*Laughter. JESUS maintains his royal composure.*)

HEROD   (*rising, indignant*) Do you mock me? —
          We shall see who plays the fool, you fraud!
          Jester, off with your robe! (*He obliges.*)
          Now put it on our distinguished guest
          so that he may play his part with proper attire.

          (JESTER *does so.* COURT *bursts into laughter.*)
          Now then, Annas, you may return him to Pilate.

161

And tell him that *that* is what his friend Herod
judges the prisoner guilty of!

☆　☆　☆

CHORUS　*I am no longer a man — just a worm:*
scorned by all, the butt of their jokes.
All who see me ridicule me.

—*Psalm 22:6,7*

FOOLS FOR CHRIST

The cross has become a symbol of triumph.
It hangs gracefully from the necks of countless Christians
and proudly crowns the steeples of our churches.
But it was not always so.
To the early Christians it was a symbol of shame.
Around the year 200 on a wall of the servants' quarters
in the emperor's palace in Rome,
a pagan page-boy drew a crude picture:
He scrawled the figure of a fellow page,
his arms raised in prayer, standing before a cross.
On the cross was a human body,
and on the body, the head of a jackass.
Below were the words: "Alexemenos adores his god."
The next time you go to church, imagine that
in place of the crucifix you're so used to seeing,
you were to see a man dangling from a noose,
or strapped in an electric chair,
or tied to the post of a firing-squad.
Your reaction?
"Who dared desecrate our church?"
Yet that's exactly what crucifixion was:
capital punishment
reserved only for slaves and common criminals.
God's only Son died that way! Why?
For you, for me, for all of us — to save us.
"Christ was sinless.
Yet for our sake God filled Him with sin,
so that we might be filled with God's goodness." (2 Co 5:21)
Are you filled with His goodness?

162

Remember, "anyone who has believed God's saving message
and then falls away
is crucifying the Son of God all over again." (Heb 6:5,6)
Are you crucifying Jesus in your life with:
Drugs? Alcohol? Impure thoughts? Illicit sex?
Stealing? Cheating on tests? Back-biting?
Sassing your parents? Ridiculing that classmate?
"Christ suffered for you
and left you an example to follow . . ." (1 Pt 2:21)
Just how does one do that?
"Whoever wishes to follow Me
must say "NO" to himself
and take up his cross every day . . ." (Lk 9:23)
So Christianity is not for quitters.
It's for the courageous —
for people like the page-boy Alexemenos,
who, in spite of ridicule,
still want to follow Our Lord.

40

An hour later. Torture room in the substructure of Pilate's residence. Enter mercenary SOLDIERS with JESUS.

Jn 19:1-3 / Mt 27:27-31

1st
SOLDIER

And now for some real entertainment —
teaching this Jew a lesson!
All right, prisoner, — strip!

(JESUS *removes his clothing.* SOLDIER *ties him
to a stone column and begins to beat him with
a whip, studded with bone-chips. Blood flies in
all directions. Flaying continues for five minutes.*)

2nd
SOLDIER

Save something for me! (JESUS *is untied, turned
around, and retied.* 2nd SOLDIER *continues the
flogging, swearing at every stroke.* JESUS *stands
in a pool of his blood.*)

CAPTAIN

He's had enough. Pilate wants him alive.

1st
SOLDIER

Wait! We can't send him away like this!
(*assumes mock-seriuos tone*) After all,
if he's their king, we should *crown* him first.

3rd
SOLDIER

Crown him? With what?

1st
SOLDIER

Bring me those thorn branches we use for kindling
and I'll show you. (3rd SOLDIER *fetches some
branches.* 1st SOLDIER *overturns a wooden tub and
seats JESUS on it. He then proceeds to entwine
the thorns around his temples.*)
His Majesty needs a royal cloak!
(*to* 3rd SOLDIER) Get me my old scarlet cape!
(*A patched-up cape is brought and flung on JESUS.*)
And one thing more — a royal scepter!

<table>
<tr><td></td><td>(He jams a reed into JESUS' hands.)
Now — his Majesty will hold court.
Courtiers, line up! (SOLDIERS fall in line.)</td></tr>
<tr><td>3rd
SOLDIER</td><td>(on both knees, in mocking tone)
Long live the king of the Jews!
(He rises slowly, then spits in JESUS' face.)</td></tr>
<tr><td>2nd
SOLDIER</td><td>Your royal Highness! (He rises and smashes
JESUS in the face with his fist.)</td></tr>
<tr><td>1st
SOLDIER</td><td>All hail, your Majesty! (He takes the reed
from JESUS and beats him on the head with it.)</td></tr>
<tr><td>CAPTAIN</td><td>(moving in) That's enough!
Pilate wants to exhibit him to the crowd.
They're clamoring for blood.
This should satisfy them.</td></tr>
</table>

☆   ☆   ☆

CHORUS *I gave no resistance.*
I did not turn away.
I offered my back to those who beat me,
my cheeks to those who tore at my beard.
I did not shield my face
from spitting and insult.

— Isaiah 50:5,6

"SUFFERED UNDER PONTIUS PILATE"

Q. Who suffered under Pontius Pilate?
A. Jesus Christ, His only Son, our Lord.
Q. Whose only Son?
A. God's only Son.
Q. Was he conscious of the suffering?
A. He was. To be unconscious is not to suffer at all.
   A patient is given an anesthetic before surgery
   to make him unconscious
   so that he feels no pain.
Q. But isn't Jesus Christ God?
A. He is. Just as much God as the Father.
Q. But God cannot suffer —

166

A. As God, He cannot suffer.
   That is why He became man,
   so that He could suffer — in His human nature.
Q. You mean, God really suffered?
A. He did.
   In Jesus there is only *one* person — a *divine* person.
   And the *person* is the one who suffers:
   "*I* have a tooth-ache . . ." "My head is killing *me*."
Q. Then God Himself really felt the pain?
A. He did.
   He really felt:
         the whips cutting His back into ribbons,
         the heavy cross lacerating His shoulder,
         the nails searing the nerve centers in His wrists,
         the thirst scorching His throat dry,
         the agony at that lonely moment of death.
   If we had been beaten and crucified,
   we would have felt it all.
   He was beaten and crucified.
   He felt it all.*
So the next time you feel tempted to sin,
consider what it cost God to save you:
"Remember, the ransom paid to free you from your sins
was not gold or silver or anything perishable,
but rather the precious blood of a spotless lamb,
Christ Himself!" (1 Pt 1:18,19)

---

* The above has been adapted from B. J. Lonergan, S.J., "Christ as Subject:
A Reply" *Gregorianum* (Rome 1959) XL, 2, pp. 265-66. Used with permission.

41

Moments later, the balcony of the Governor's palace. PILATE enters and motions for silence.

Jn 19:4-16 / Mk 15:6-15

PILATE
: I have had the prisoner whipped.
I now bring him out to you
so that you may see for yourselves.

(Enter JESUS wearing the crown of thorns and the mock-royal cloak.)

Behold the man!

JEWISH LEADERS
: Away with him! Away with him!

(The MOB takes up the refrain. PILATE deliberates, then motions for silence.)

PILATE
: At Passover we have the tradition
of releasing whichever prisoner you choose.
There's a certain Barabbas, locked-up for murder!
And here is Jesus — your would-be king!
Now which one should I release for you?

(The JEWISH LEADERS have been moving frantically, prompting the CROWD.)

CROWD
: Barabbas! We want Barabbas!

PILATE
: What, then, am I to do with your king?

CROWD
: Crucify him! Crucify him!

PILATE
: *(exasperated) You* be the ones to crucify him!
I judge him not guilty.

CAIPHAS
: We have a law that says he must die
for claiming to be the Son of God!

(PILATE takes JESUS inside and seats himself.)

168

PILATE   Where do you come from? (*Silence*)
No answer, prisoner?
Are you not aware that I have it in my power
to set you free — or to hang you from a cross?!

JESUS   You would have no power over me at all,
if it had not been given to you from above.
However, you are less at fault
than the one who turned me over to you.

(PILATE *leads* JESUS *out to the balcony again.*)

PILATE   I have again examined the prisoner
and my judgement remains the same:
He ought to go free.

CAIPHAS   If you release this man,
you are no friend of Caesar's.
Anyone who makes himself king is opposing Caesar.

(PILATE *motions for the tribunal-seat to be
brought out. When it is in place, he sits.*)

PILATE   For the last time I present him to you — your king!

CROWD   Away with him! Crucify him! Crucify him!

PILATE   (*with bitter sarcasm*) What!
Your own *king* you want me to crucify?

CROWD   We have no king but Caesar!

PILATE   (*weary*) Very well. As you wish.
Take him away!

☆   ☆   ☆

CHORUS   *The leaders of Israel said to Samuel:*
"We want a king like the other nations have."
Then the Lord said to Samuel:
"Give them their king.
You are not the one they have rejected.
They have rejected me as their king."
            — 1 Samuel 8:4-7

CRIMINALS VERSUS THE CRADLE

"No, not Jesus! We want Barabbas!" (Jn 18:40)
We need not condemn the callousness of that mob.
We moderns are still exonerating hardened criminals,
while we clamor for innocent blood
by defending abortion-on-demand.
How can one grasp the evil of abortion?
We condemn the Nazis for exterminating six million Jews.
Yet our own government calmly reports that legal abortions
in America have surpassed that figure as of December '77.
We condemn the ancient Romans and their vomitoriums:
Eat, tickle the throat, vomit, go back, eat some more!
Which is worse: that disgusting orgy
or wrenching a helpless baby from the womb
with a vacuum cleaner —
only to continue ones' irresponsible behavior?
The pro-abortionists object:
"The Supreme Court said it's difficult to say
when human life begins . . ."
Then the Court's ruling was a travesty of justice.
Cases of doubt must be resolved in favor of human life:
If you're not sure it's a deer or a hunter in the bush,
in conscience you cannot pull the trigger.
The pro-abortionists counter with: *"Wait!*
Abortion terminates a pregnancy — not a human life!"
Fine-sounding words to cloak one's conscience!
It's biology — not theology — that teaches us:
"At 4 weeks the baby's heart is beating.
At 6 weeks all major organs are formed and functioning.
At 8 weeks the baby responds to noise and touch.
At 12 weeks he sucks his thumb and feels pain."
Most abortions are performed
when the unborn baby is 9 to 12 weeks old!
Abortionists: *"A woman can do what she wants with her body."*
A woman should control herself *before* pregnancy.
After pregnancy results,
there is another body that must be considered.
Besides, St. Paul reminds us: "Don't you know

170

that your body is a temple of the Holy Spirit?
You do not belong to yourselves but to God." (1 Co 6:19)
Abortionists: *"Who cares? It's still legal."*
True. And it was also legal to kill
Jews in Germany,
baby-boys in Bethlehem,
and Christ on Calvary.

42

Noon. Calvary, a small hill outside Jerusalem's Ephraim gate. The execution party arrives: JESUS, TWO THIEVES, SOLDIERS, accompanied by PRIESTS, SCRIBES AND CURIOSITY-SEEKERS.

Jn 19:16-32 / Mt 27:32-50 / Lk 23:39-47

CENTURION
Soldiers, help the criminals
unload the cross-beams from their backs!

CHORUS
Abraham loaded the wood for the sacrifice on Isaac.
The boy said: "Father, we have fire and wood,
but where is the lamb for the sacrifice?"
Abraham answered: "My son, God Himself
will provide the lamb for the sacrifice."
(Gn 22:6-8)

☆   ☆   ☆

CENTURION
Now strip the criminals of their clothing!
(*JESUS' inner garment clings to his wounds.*
As it is pulled off, the wounds reopen raw.)
Set them down on the cross-beams,
and get busy with those hammers!

CHORUS
They dig holes in my hands and my feet —
I can count my bones one by one. (Ps 22:16)

☆   ☆   ☆

JESUS
(*while the nails are driven through his wrists*)
Father, forgive them;
they do not know what they are doing.

With great exertion TWO SOLDIERS *raise the*
crossbeam to the top of the vertical, which is
already fixed in the ground. 1st SOLDIER *bends*
JESUS' *knees while* 2nd SOLDIER *nails the*

172

superimposed feet flat against the cross. Enter —
JESUS' MOTHER, JOHN, MARY
MAGDALENE, *and* SALOME. *Crushed with grief,*
his MOTHER *watches the proceedings.*

CHORUS   *O all you who pass this way,*
stop and see
if there is any sorrow like my sorrow. (Lam 1:12)

☆   ☆   ☆

1st SOLDIER *nails the crime-placard over* JESUS.
It reads: "JESUS OF NAZARETH, KING OF
THE JEWS."

3rd
SOLDIER   Mark, hurry — we're ready to divide the spoils.
(He takes JESUS' *tunic and tears in into four*
pieces.)

2nd
SOLDIER   Look! There are no seams in the robe.
It's one solid weave. Let's not tear it.
Why not roll dice for it to see who gets it?

CHORUS   *They divide my garments among them,*
and for my clothing they cast lots. (Ps 22:18)

☆   ☆   ☆

SCRIBE   So you were going to destroy the Temple
and rebuild it in three days!
Well come down from that cross and save yourself!

ANNAS   Look at him!
He saved others, but cannot save himself.
Let our so-called Messiah come down from the
cross and then we'll believe in him!

CHORUS   *All who see me ridicule me.*
They wag their heads and sneer at me:
"He trusted in the Lord,
so let the Lord save him now." (Ps 22:8)

☆   ☆   ☆

1st
THIEF   Are you the Messiah?
Well then, save yourself and us, too!

173

2nd THIEF	Don't you fear God at all? We deserve our punishment but he is innocent — Jesus, remember me when you enter your kingdom.
JESUS	This very day you shall be with me in paradise.
CHORUS	*He was buried with the wicked.* (Is 53:9)

☆   ☆   ☆

Two more hours pass slowly. The sun gradually darkens as during an eclipse. JESUS looks down at his MOTHER, standing next to JOHN.

JESUS	Woman, there is your son. — (*looking at* JOHN) There is your mother.
CHORUS	*The Lord God said to the serpent:* *"I will make enemies of you and the woman —* *of your offspring and her offspring.* *He will crush your head,* *while you strike at his heel."* (Gn 3:15)

☆   ☆   ☆

JESUS	My God, my God, why have you abandoned me? (*He pauses and looks at the BYSTANDERS.*) I'm dying of thirst!
1st SOLDIER	Poor man! — Here, let's soak this sponge in some wine. (*He raises the sponge on a reed to JESUS' lips.*)
JESUS	It is now finished! (*He raises his eyes to heaven.*) Father, into Your hands I entrust my spirit. (*He bows his head and dies. Peals of thunder begin rolling. The earth begins to quake. The BYSTANDERS shout in panic.*)
CENTURION	This man must have been God's son!
CHORUS	*My God, my God, why have You abandoned me?* *All day long I call out, but You do not answer.* *My strength has drained away like water,* *my bones are all pulled loose,*

my heart has melted like wax,
my mouth is parched dry,
my tongue sticks to my lips.
You have left me here in the dust of death!
— *Psalm 22:1,2,14,15*

THE NEW ADAM AND THE NEW EVE

"Beneath the cross of Jesus stood his Mother." (Jn 19:25)
That was no place for a woman to be, much less a mother.
Why, then, was Mary there?
And why does Jesus call His own Mother "Woman"?
The answer is not easily perceived by the worldly.
For the title "Woman" was first uttered in another garden.
(In v. 41, St. John expressly states:
"There was a garden in the place where he was crucified.")
In the first garden, there was another tree —
"the tree of the knowledge of good and evil" (Gn 2:16),
now replaced by the tree between the good and evil thief.
The fruit of the first tree, "so pleasant to behold" (Gn 3:6),
is supplanted by the blessed fruit of Mary's womb.
Through the tree in Eden, the first Adam disobeyed God
and "caused sin and death to enter the world." (Rm 5:12)
The second Adam, Jesus, restored life when He became
"obedient unto death — even the death on a cross." (Phl 2:8)
Under the first tree Eve cooperated in man's downfall:
"The woman took the fruit, ate, and gave it to her husband."
Beneath the cross of Jesus stood Mary, —
the second Eve, cooperating in our redemption.
In Eden, God had told the first woman:
"You will bear your children in pain and sorrow." (Gn 3:16)
The second Eve had heard a similar prediction from Simeon:
"A sword of sorrow shall pierce your heart . . ." (Lk 2:35) —
a prediction which was fulfilled on Calvary,
when she bore her offspring in great anguish.
In Eden, God had declared war between Satan and "the WOMAN
between your seed and her seed . . ." (Gn 3:15)
On Calvary, Jesus revealed that Mary was that Woman:
"WOMAN, there is your son" — your offspring, John —

175

who at that moment, represented all true believers in Christ.
Jesus had called Mary WOMAN only once before — at Cana,
when He hesistated at first to perform the miracle,
giving as His reason:
"WOMAN, my hour has not yet come." (Jn 2:4)
Now that His hour had come at last — His hour of glory —
He again addressed her as WOMAN,
thereby informing her that she could now request of Him
anything she wished on behalf of her needy offspring.
Years later, St. John, who had been present
on both occasions when Mary was called WOMAN,
had a stupendous vision:
"A great sign appeared in the heavens,
a WOMAN dressed in the sun, with the moon under her feet,
and a crown of twelve stars on her head.
She was about to give birth to a son . . .
In front of the WOMAN there stood a great dragon —
that ancient serpent, called the Devil or Satan,
waiting to devour her child.
She gave birth to a son, who was taken to God's throne.
Then the WOMAN fled to the desert,
to be cared for in a special place for 1,260 days.
The dragon was furious with the WOMAN
and went off to wage war on the *rest of her children,*
that is, on those who obey God's commandments
and who follow Jesus." (Rv ch. 12)
And so from that momentous hour, when Jesus told John,
"There is your Mother",
we have the right — as Mary's children —
to run to her for protection
in our relentless war with her ancient enemy — the Serpent!

43 | Calvary, an hour later. BYSTANDERS and SOLDIERS remain posted beneath the crosses. Enter SOLDIER wielding a club. He begins to batter the legs of the 1st THIEF amid cries of agony.

Jn 19:31-42

SCRIBE   Soldier, what are you up to?

SOLDIER   Pilate's orders.
He wants the bodies buried by sundown.
With their legs broken,
they won't be able to lift themselves up
to ease the pressure on their lungs.
They'll suffocate in no time. (*He breaks
the legs of the* 2nd THIEF *and turns to* JESUS.)

CENTURION   Save your strength, soldier.
He's already dead.

SOLDIER   In that case, hand me your spear.
I have to be sure — (*He pierces* JESUS' *side.*)
Strange! What do you make of that?
Blood and water!

Shortly, enter JOSEPH OF ARIMETHEA *with*
NICODEMUS *and* ASSISTANTS, *carrying*
ointments and burial shroud.
JOSEPH *approaches the* CENTURION.

JOSEPH   Sir, I have Pilate's permission to bury the body.
Here is the notice in his own hand.
I own a tomb in the garden
on the other side of the hill.
We'll bury him there.

177

CENTURION   Very well, — you may proceed.

*The body is removed from the cross, washed,
and wrapped in the shroud. It is reverently
carried off for burial.*

☆   ☆   ☆

CHORUS   *Then the Lord God put Adam into a deep sleep.
And while he slept,
God took a rib from his side
and formed it into a woman
and presented her to Adam.*

— *Genesis 2:21,22*

THE BRIDE OF CHRIST

We have already seen how St. Paul referred to the Church
as the Mystical Body of Christ. (Scene 33)
In his letter to the Ephesians,
he makes another beautiful comparison: *the Bride of Christ.*
"Husbands, love your wives, just as Christ loved the Church
and gave Himself up for her . . ." (Eph 5:25)
In Revelation 21, St. John takes up the same theme:
"Then one of the seven angels said to me,
'Come, and I will show you the bride, the wife of the Lamb.'
Then he showed me the Holy City Jerusalem (= the Church)
coming down out of heaven from God,
beautiful as a bride ready to meet her husband." (vv. 9,10,2)
John had witnessed the actual wedding ceremony years before
"when the Lamb of God (to use St. Augustine's words)
mounted the marriage bed of the Cross —
with His arms outstretched to embrace us,
His head bowed to kiss us,
His side pierced to receive us!
He lovingly gave Himself up
and forever joined Himself with the WOMAN,
His spotless Bride, the Church . . ."
Then, as He fell into the deep sleep of death,
His side — like Adam's was opened,
and from that side flowed blood and water,

178

symbols of the chief sacraments
that would nourish His beautiful Bride:
the waters of Baptism and the Eucharistic Blood!
There were other sacraments that He left His Bride,
visible tokens of His love for Her.
For basically that is what a sacrament is:
a visible sign
given to us by Christ
to communicate divine life (= *sanctifying grace*).
There are seven such signs — seven sacraments —
each corresponding to a different stage of spiritual growth.
For as in the case with the natural body,
the Mystical Body, too, develops in an orderly sequence.
Their stages of development may be shown thus:

NATURAL BODY	MYSTICAL BODY	INSTITUTED BY CHRIST
1. We are born.	Baptism	Mt 28:19
2. We need food.	Eucharist	1 Co 11:23-26
3. We mature.	Confirmation	Ac 8:14-17
4. We marry.	Marriage	1 Co 7:10
5. We seek pardon.	Penance	Jn 20:22,23
6. We take medicine.	Holy Anointing	Jm 5:14,15 (Mk 5:13)
7. We are governed.	Holy Orders	Lk 22:19 (Ac 13:2,3)

44

Early morning, two days later. Jerusalem, the upper room, where TEN DISCIPLES are scattered about. SEVERAL hold their heads buried in their hands; OTHERS stare blankly ahead. The death-like stillness is broken by loud pounding.

Jn 20:1,2 / Mk 16:1-4

MAGDALENE   (*knocking frantically*) John, open the door!

(JOHN *crosses to the door and unbolts it.*
Enter MARY MAGDALENE, *breathless.*)

They've taken the body from the tomb —
and we don't know where they have put it!

JOHN   Impossible! What makes you say that?

MAGDALENE   This morning before dawn —
Salome and James' mother and I
bought more spices to finish the embalming. —
On the way to the tomb we kept wondering
how to roll back the stone from the entrance.
But when we arrived —
the stone was already rolled *far back!* —
We went inside —
but the body was *gone!!*

PETER   Gone? Who could have taken it?

JOHN   I don't know, Simon. Let's go see for ourselves.

Exit PETER *and* JOHN *running.*

☆   ☆   ☆

CHORUS   *And so, my heart and soul rejoice;*
my body, too, rests in peace.
For you will not abandon me among the dead.
nor allow the one you love to see corruption.
         — *Psalm 16:9,10*

THE RESURRECTION: A HOAX?

Who discovered America?
Were you there when Columbus stepped ashore?
Then how can you be certain that he did?
By taking the word of others:
    of the sailors who accompanied him,
    of the mate who kept the log,
    of the Spanish court who received the gold
    and alien products (tobacco, maize) from the New World.
In short,
all belief is founded on the word of reliable witnesses!
So how can we be sure that Jesus rose from the dead?
By taking the word of those who saw Him alive again.
In the words of Peter to the household of Cornelius:
"We are witnesses to everything that Jesus did . . .
They killed him by nailing him to a cross,
but God raised him to life on the third day
and allowed him to appear, not to everyone,
but to certain chosen witnessses.
Yes, we are the chosen witnesses who ate and drank with him
after he rose from the dead . . ." (Ac 10:39-41)
Is it possible that the disciples
contrived the resurrection story to deceive us? —
That Jesus never really rose from the dead at all?
Suppose for a moment that such was the case.
Then we must reason as follows:
If they went so far to fabricate such a colossal lie,
why didn't they embellish it with more convincing details?
1. On the day of the resurrection, the *men* are hiding
   behind locked doors in deadly fear of the authorities.
   Why "make up" such a humiliating incident?
2. The *women* are the first to discover the empty tomb,
   and Mary Magdalene is the first to see the risen Lord.
   But in the official list of appearances in 1 Co 15:5-8,
   the women are not even mentioned! Why?
   Because female testimony was not valid in Jewish courts!
   Yet all four gospels put the women at the tomb *first*.
   Why "add" such an unnecessary item to their story?

3. On learning of the empty tomb,
   Mary Magdalene and the disciples concluded:
   "Someone has stolen the body!"
   Their first thought was not of a resurrection! (Jn 20:9)
   Why put on their own lips the very charge
   that the High Priests were to make of them:
   "Say that his disciples came during the night
   and stole the body . . ."? (Mt 28:13)
   Since they were "fabricating" the resurrection,
   why not say that they were expecting it,
   to conform with Jesus' three predictions of the event?

4. Far from expecting the resurrection, the disciples
   had to be persuaded that it was really Jesus
   through many appearances under various circumstances,
   as we shall see in the remaining sections.
   Again, why "include" so many embarrassing details,
   if such were not really the case?

The thinking person must surely ask himself:
Would the apostles have laid down their lives
for a cruel hoax which they themselves had invented?
With the exception of St. John, they all died as martyrs
in witness to the truth of what they were preaching.
An anonymous author drew the only conclusion possible:
"Think of the psychological absurdity
of picturing a little band of defeated cowards
cowering in an upper room one day
and a few days later transformed into a company
that no persecution could silence —
and then attempting to attribute this dramatic change
to nothing more than a miserable fabrication
they were trying to foist upon the world.
That simply would not make sense."

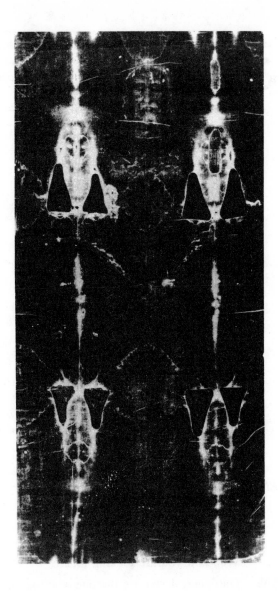

45

The tomb, fifteen minutes later. Enter JOHN panting. He crouches to peer inside. Enter PETER breathless. He enters the tomb; JOHN follows.

Jn 20:3-18

PETER
John, the body *is* gone!
But look — the burial shroud is still here.

JOHN
But why is it folded?
And the head-band is folded, too!
I fastened that around his head myself!

PETER
Strange!
Why would a thief waste time folding the linens?

JOHN
For that matter,
why would a thief have left the linens behind?

Exit PETER and JOHN, shaking their heads. A few minutes later, enter MARY MAGDALENE sobbing. She sits at the entrance to the tomb. peering inside, she sees two ANGELS in white robes, sitting at each end of the slab where the body of Jesus had been.

ANGEL
Woman, why are you crying?

MAGDALENE
They have taken my Lord away
and I don't know where they have put him.

(*Enter JESUS behind MARY MAGDALENE.*)

JESUS
Woman, why those tears?
Who is it you are looking for?

MAGDALENE
Gardener, if you are the one who took him away,
please tell me where I can find him.

JESUS
Mary!

MAGDALENE   My Master! (*She embraces his feet.*)
JESUS   Do not hold on to me.
            I have not yet ascended to the Father.
            But go to my disciples and tell them
            that I am returning to my Father,
            who is now your Father —
            the very one you call your God.

☆   ☆   ☆

CHORUS   *I met the watchmen on their rounds*
            and asked them, "Have you seen my beloved?"
            No sooner had I left them, than I found him.
            I held him and would not let him go.
                            — Song of Songs 3:3-4

A SKEPTIC'S SEARCH

by Carl Hiaasen

The image on the ancient burial linen belonged to a thin, bearded man. He had a long aquiline nose and wore his hair down to his shoulders. He was nude and had been tortured savagely before his death on a cross.

Nails had been driven through both wrists. He had been beaten in the face, stabbed in the chest and flogged with a whip studded with dog's teeth. A small cap of thorns had cut into his forehead.

Is this the image of Jesus Christ? Since it surfaced more than six centuries ago in Europe, the Sacred Shroud of Turin, Italy, has been accepted by many theologians as authentic . . .

Miami reporter Robert Wilcox first heard of the shroud four years ago after he suddenly found himself promoted to religion editor of the *Miami News*. A veteran crime reporter and hardened religious skeptic (he still does not attend church), Wilcox was fascinated with the photographic quality of the image on the shroud.

In 1973 he spent his vacation in Turin, where he was one of a very few given permission to examine the closely guarded 14-foot length of herringbone twill. Upon returning to the States, he promptly quit his job to work on the shroud story.

185

Wilcox thought he could explain the image as some sort of chemical stain, and the body as merely one of many Roman crucifixion victims.

He began his odyssey by sorting through 2,000 burial cloths in the Louvre, hoping to find a comparable phenomenon. He could not. For two years he crisscrossed Europe and the U.S. quizzing historians and scientists who might be able to offer an explanation.

None could, and Wilcox was still baffled when he sat down to write the story. His book, *Shroud,* was published in October by Macmillan and is now headed for a third printing. It is stirring up intense new curiosity about Italy's famous religious relic.

Wilcox was two-thirds through the manuscript before admitting he had been convinced, "This cloth," he says, "wrapped the historical person Jesus. I think I proved that."

Although no one can suggest how it got there, few experts dispute that the image on the shroud is that of a human corpse in rigor mortis. The question has always been: Whose image is it and how did the fabric survive intact almost 2,000 years?

While the shroud can conclusively be traced back as far as 1354, Wilcox contends it is mentioned in literature as early as the fifth century. Recent evidence — traces of certain pollens found on the shroud — place it in Palestine roughly at the time of Christ.

Furthermore, details imprinted on the shroud — such as abrasions on the shoulder of the victim, the thorn lacerations and the lance wound — seem uncannily to match the Bible's description of Christ's crucifixion.

Still, the most puzzling mystery is how such a chilling image was imprinted on fabric. Wilcox believes it occurred during a supernatural blast of heat or light at the instant of the Resurrection.

Those who have seen it describe the image as faint but discernible to the naked eye. The physiological details become visible only when negatives of shroud photographs are examined.

Wilcox grudgingly discarded his doubts as he finished writing the final chapters of *Shroud.* Periodically, he would stop typing to stare at a picture hanging in his Coconut Grove study — the bearded visage burned on the Shroud of Turin. "It had a religious effect on me," he conceded. "It's material evidence. That's the face of Jesus."

Reprinted with permission from *US* Magazine (488 Madison Ave., New York, N.Y.) Jan. 24, 1978, p. 29.

46

Late that same afternoon. On the Joppa road from Jerusalem, two disciples, CLEO-PAS and SIMEON, are nearing the village of Emmaus.

Lk 24:13-32

CLEOPAS   Last week it was "Hosanna to the Son of David!"
and today — dead and gone!

SIMEON   The cures! The miracles! And to end like this!

(*Enter* JESUS. *They do not recognize him.*)

JESUS   Why are you two so sad?

CLEOPAS   Sir, are you the only one in all Jerusalem
who hasn't heard what happened?

JESUS   Heard what happened?

CLEOPAS   To Jesus, the holy prophet from Nazareth —
a great miracle-worker and a fearless preacher.
Our religious leaders had him crucified
just as he was about to liberate Israel.

JESUS   And when did all of this take place?

CLEOPAS   The day before yesterday.
Besides, some women from our group have us puzzled.
They were at his tomb this morning
and reported that his body was gone.
They said some angels had told them he was alive.
Two of our men went out to check,
and sure enough, the body was missing,
just as the women had said.

JESUS   O how slow you are to believe the prophets of old!
Was it not predicted that the Messiah had to suffer
before entering into his glory?

187

CLEOPAS	Had to suffer?
JESUS	Recall the Suffering Servant in Isaiah: "Ours were the sufferings he endured, ours the pains he bore. He was wounded for our sins, and tortured for our evil deeds."
CLEOPAS	The suffering servant . . .?
JESUS	And what else is David's psalm but a description of the Messiah's death? "They dig holes in my hands and my feet, I can count my bones one by one . . ."
SIMEON	Cleopas, — wake up. We're in the village —
CLEOPAS	Surely, sir, you will spend the night with us. It's already close to sundown.
	They enter the house, wash their hands, and sit at table. JESUS *takes the bread, looks up to heaven, and breaks it.*
JESUS	Father, Lord of heaven and earth, I thank You for . . .
CLEOPAS	*Jesus!!*
SIMEON	*Master!!* (JESUS *vanishes.*)
CLEOPAS	He's alive! No wonder my heart was on fire while he was explaining the Scriptures to us!
SIMEON	So was mine! Let's hurry back to tell the others.

☆　　☆　　☆

CHORUS	*After all his suffering, my Servant shall be clothed in light. I shall grant him a place among the mighty.*

— Isaiah 53:11-12

188

NO CROSS, NO CROWN

"The Messiah had to suffer before entering his glory."
Growth in life usually implies some form of suffering:
"A woman about to give birth suffers pain . . ." (Jn 16:21)
If this is true of our bodies,
much more so is it of our souls.
"My dear children, I am suffering birth-pangs for you,
so that Christ may be formed in you." (Ga 4:19)
When God sends the cross into our lives —
 the loss of a loved one,
 an incurable disease,
 some emotional disorder, —
if we rebel against Him,
we are disowning Him as our Father. (Heb 12:5-13)
If we welcome the cross,
we become living patterns of His Son.
That's what St. Paul meant in Col 1:24:
"I complete in my own body
what Christ still has to suffer in His Body — the Church."
According to Dr. Viktor Frankl, ". . . man's main concern
is not to gain pleasure or to avoid pain,
but rather to see a meaning in his life.
That is why man is even ready to suffer,
on the condition . . . that his suffering has meaning,
such as the meaning of a sacrifice . . ."*
So the first thing on rising each day,
give your day meaning by making the *Morning Offering:*
"O Jesus, through Mary's Immaculate Heart,
this day I offer You
all my prayers and actions,
all my joys and sufferings.
I do so for my own past sins and those of others,
and for all the desires of Your most Sacred Heart."

---

* *Man's Search for Meaning.* Pocket Books (N.Y. 1973) p. 179.

☆ ☆ ☆

During World War I Joyce Kilmer saw in his daily hardships reflections of the sufferings of Christ:

PRAYER OF A SOLDIER IN FRANCE

My shoulders ache beneath my pack
(Lie easier, Cross, upon His back).
I march with feet that burn and smart
(Tread, Holy Feet, upon my heart).
Men shout at me who may not speak
(They scourged Thy back and smote Thy cheek).
I may not lift a hand to clear
My eyes of salty drops that sear.
(Then shall my fickle soul forget
Thy Agony of bloody sweat?)
My rifle hand is stiff and numb
(From Thy pierced palm red rivers come).
Lord, Thou didst suffer more for me
Than all the hosts of land and sea.
So let me render back again
This millionth of Thy gift. Amen.

<table>
<tr><td>

47
</td><td>

Jerusalem, the upper room, two hours later. TEN DISCIPLES are scattered in small groups. Loud pounding interrupts their discussions.
</td></tr>
</table>

Lk 24:33-43 / Jn 20:19-25

MATTHEW (*crossing to door*) Who is it?

CLEOPAS Cleopas and Simeon. Hurry — open! (MATTHEW *unbolts the door, they enter, he rebolts it.*)
He's ALIVE! We saw him ourselves!
He broke bread for us in Emmaus.

SIMEON On the way, he explained all the Scriptures,
telling us why he had to suffer and die.
But we didn't recognize him until . . .

JAMES Calm down! You sound delirious!

(*Suddenly, through the closed doors enter* JESUS)

JESUS Peace to all of you.

PHILIP Heaven save us? It's his ghost!

JESUS Why are you so upset and doubtful?
Here, look at my hands and my feet.
Touch me, and see that I am real.
A ghost does not have flesh and bones as I have.
(DISCIPLES *gather around, still incredulous.*)
Do you have anything here to eat?

PHILIP Yes, some broiled fish.

(*He gives some to* JESUS, *who eats it.
When he finishes, he looks at them solemnly.*)

JESUS The Father has sent me into the world,
now I am sending you. (*He breathes on them.*)

Receive the Holy Spirit.
The sins that you forgive, will be forgiven.
The sins you do not forgive, will still remain.

(*He vanishes.*)

DISCIPLES   (*together*) It was the Lord!
       He's alive!
       Seems too good to be true!

(*There is a knock at the door.*)

JOHN   Who's there?

THOMAS   The Twin! (JOHN *unbolts the door. Enter* THOMAS.)

JOHN   You missed him, Thomas! We just saw the Lord!

THOMAS   I don't believe it!

PHILIP   But we *did* see him.
At first we thought it was his ghost.
I even touched his hand when he took . . .

THOMAS   (*deliberately*) You are all going mad.

DISCIPLES   (*together*) No, Thomas, it *was* the Lord!
We saw him!
He came right through the bolted doors.
He even ate some of the fish we had for supper!

THOMAS   Just who do you take me for?
I'm not believing a thing
until I can see the nail-wounds in his hands
and put my finger in them —
and put my hand right into his side!

☆   ☆   ☆

CHORUS   *If anyone should ask him,*
"What are these wounds in your hands?"
he will reply, "These are the wounds
that I received in the house of my friends."
          — Zechariah 13:6

192

PARDON AND PEACE

"Who can forgive sins but God alone?" (Mk 2:7)
The scribes first voiced that complaint against Jesus.
Since then, it has been raised many times
against those who forgive sins in the name of Jesus.
"I don't need a priest to forgive my sins.
I confess my sins to God alone.
I've offended Him, so He's the only One who can forgive me."
Why, then, does the Church insist we confess to a priest?
Because that's how Jesus set up the Sacrament of Penance.
St. John records the actual words of institution:
"The sins that you forgive, will be forgiven.
The sins you do not forgive, will still remain." (20:23)
How does that text prove the necessity of confessing sins?
Let's answer that question by asking another one.
How does a court judge find a person quilty or innocent?
By looking at the accused in the eyes?
Or by examining the evidence and then deciding?
So, too, in the confessional,
before a priest can pass sentence,
he must know if the penitent is sorry or not.
If there is true sorrow
(*"Yes, Father, I'll stop seeing that married woman."*),
reconciliation can follow.
If there is no sign of sorrow
(*"No, Father, I won't pay back what I took."*),
then forgiveness is not possible.
So you see, the words of Jesus Himself show
that the actual sins are to be mentioned
before they can be forgiven in the Sacrament of Penance.
Unfortunately, many people become somewhat irrational
in dealing with this sacrament.
They fail to realize that the most important factor
is not the mere recital of a list of sins,
but rather the *sorrow* that must be present for those sins.
For Jesus is always ready to forgive us
provided we are sorry.
He gave us this sacrament,

193

not to add another burden to our already burdened lives,
but as a means of achieving great peace.
The circumstances under which He instituted it prove that.
It was on Easter Sunday night
when He came through the closed doors of the upper room.
As Father Alfred Wilson, C.P. pointed out,
this was His first meeting with His chosen band
since His arrest in the garden on Holy Thursday.
What would *you* have said under those circumstances?
"So there you are, Peter! You don't know who I am, do you?
And you, Philip, James, Matthew — and the rest of you —
fine friends you turned out to be!
You deserted me — just when I needed you most!"
No — not a word of their treachery.
Just a greeting of peace!
And then He bestowed on them His sacrament of Peace,
the sacrament of Reconciliation (or Penance).
So it's sad to hear Catholics complain,
"Why do they make us go to Confession?"
We see a dentist twice a year
and a doctor at the first sign of illness.
Which is more important:
the health of our bodies
or the well-being of our immortal souls?

48

Late evening, one week later. The ELEVEN DISCIPLES are gathered in the upper room. Enter JESUS through the bolted doors.

Jn 20:26-31

JESUS
: Peace to all of you. (*He looks around.*)
Thomas, come here. (THOMAS *approaches with hesitation.* JESUS *takes his hand and guides it.*)
Put your finger into my hands —
and put your hand into my side.
Now stop doubting — and believe!

THOMAS
: (*falling to his knees*) My Lord and my God!

JESUS
: You believe because you have seen me.
How blessed are the ones who do not see,
and still believe!

☆ ☆ ☆

CHORUS
: *Woe is me! I am doomed.*
For I am a man of unclean lips,
and yet my eyes have seen the Lord of Hosts!
— Isaiah 6:5

THE RISEN LORD: A HALLUCINATION?

We have already ruled out the resurrection as a hoax
invented by the disciples. (Section 44)
But could the disciples themselves have been deluded?
This suggestion is a favorite ploy of modern critics:
"After the death of their beloved master,
the disciples began to reflect on his good life
and especially on the beautiful teachings he had left them.
These — they concluded — could never die.

195

Suddenly, they imagined that they saw Jesus with them again.
Yes! He was still alive — He had risen!
Such was the effect of auto-suggestion
on the emotionally-drained minds of these simple fishermen.
The resurrection was nothing more than a hallucination."
That an individual could suffer from such a delusion
is conceivable.
That all the apostles and hundreds of disciples (1 Co 15:6)
could have been thus deluded is impossible.
Furthermore, such a theory denies the scriptual evidence:

Jn 20:9   The disciples were not expecting the resurrection.
Mk 16:1   The women had set out to embalm the body.
Jn 20:2   Magdelene concluded that the body had been stolen.
Lk 24:21 The disciples of Emmaus thought he was still dead.
Lk 24:37 The disciples thought they were seeing a ghost.
Jn 20:25 Thomas withheld belief until he touched the wounds.

But even assuming that those who had known Jesus in life
were hallucinating (an impossible assumption!),
how are we to explain the case of ST. PAUL?!
He had never seen the Lord in His earthly life,
and he harbored no love for Him or His teachings.
Yet one day he is going about stamping out the hated sect,
and the next, he is a member and its chief proponent!
(Imagine an Adolf Hitler plotting to wipe out all Jews,
when he suddenly converts to Judaism!)
What caused St. Paul to change?
He claimed that he had seen the risen Lord! (1 Co 15:8)
Was he merely hallucinating?
Being a strict Pharisee (Ac 23:6),
he believed in the *physical* resurrection of the body
on the last day. (Ac 23:8)
So when Paul proclaimed that Jesus was risen —
he meant that Jesus' *physical body had returned to life!*
And Paul — the former arch-enemy of Christianity —
gave his life as a witness to what he had seen!

49

Dawn, two weeks later. SEVEN APOSTLES are aboard a small boat on the Sea of Galilee, not far from shore, where JESUS stands unnoticed.

Jn 21:1-25

PETER	Another wasted night!
JESUS	(*calling from the shore*) Have you caught anything?
JAMES	Not a thing!
JESUS	Then cast your net to the right for a catch!
	(APOSTLES *cast the net, which is filled at once.*)
JOHN	Simon, it's the Lord!
	PETER *dives into the water and swims ashore. The* OTHERS *row the boat in, dragging the net. On shore* JESUS *has lit a fire with some bread on it.*
JESUS	Bring some of the fish you just caught, and come, eat your breakfast. (*He cooks the fish and serves it with some bread.* ALL *sit around eating. When they are finished, they rise.* JESUS *takes* PETER *aside.*) Simon, son of John, do you love me more than these others do?
PETER	Yes, Lord, you know that I love you.
JESUS	Then take care of my lambs. (*brief pause*) Simon, do you really love me?
PETER	Yes, Lord, you know I do!
JESUS	Be the shepherd of my sheep. (*brief pause*) Simon, are you sure that you love me?
PETER	(*upset*) Lord, you know *everything!* You *know* that I love you!

197

JESUS	Take care of my sheep. When you were young, you would dress for a journey and go wherever you wanted to. But when you are old, someone else will bind you hand and foot, and take you where you do not want to go. Come, Simon, follow me.
PETER	(*turning, sees* JOHN) Lord, what about him?
JESUS	If I want him to stay here until I return, why should that concern you? *You* are to follow me!

☆　　☆　　☆

CHORUS	*Then I will put one shepherd over them —* *my servant David.* *He shall feed them and be their shepherd.* *I, the Lord, will be their God.* *and my servant David will be their leader.*

— Ezekiel 34:23,24

THE CHIEF SHEPHERD

In the O.T. God is the Shepherd of Israel:
"The Lord is my Shepherd . . ." (Ps 23:1)
In Jn 10, Jesus declared, "I am the Good Shepherd . . .
there will be one flock with ONE shepherd"
In Jn 21, Jesus asks Simon Peter three times if he loves him.
At each affirmation of love, Jesus orders him:
"Feed my lambs — Be shepherd to my sheep."
What did the Lord mean by that command?
Why is Peter singled out from the other disciples?
("Simon, do you love me more than *these?*")
Why is he preferred even to the beloved John?
("If I want *him* to remain . . . *you* follow me.")
And since the sheep still belong to Jesus ("*my* sheep"),
why must Peter act as their shepherd?
In the context, only one answer is possible:
The Supreme Shepherd is about to leave His flock,
but He will not leave it to the mercy of the wolves.

In His place He leaves a substitute shepherd,
who must care for the entire flock with the same love
that inspired the Supreme Shepherd.
Peter is to be Christ's replacement ("Vicar" in Latin)
and the visible head of the entire Church on earth!
(It would be helpful to review section 19 at this point.)
The other disciples recognized Peter as their leader:
His name heads all four lists of the apostles. (cf Mk 3:16)
His name occurs more than all the other eleven combined!
The first half of Acts reads more like his biography.
True, the second half concentrates on Paul,
but Paul himself recognized Peter's superiority:
1) Paul never calls him by his given name, "Simon",
but only by his functional name, "the ROCK" (Kephas).
2) How explain Peter's supporters in Corinth (1 Co 1:12),
if he, like Christ, had never set foot there?
Evidently, he must have held a unique position in the Church!
3) For Paul, the highest norm of behavior for Christians
(next to Christ Himself) is Peter! (1 Co 9:5)
4) Why did Paul, while in Jerusalem, spend two weeks
consulting with Peter, but only seeing James? (Ga 1:18-20)
5) Why such emphasis on rebuking Peter to his face? (Ga 2:11)
(From this, some conclude that Peter was inferior to Paul.)
Barnabas had also been in the wrong,
but only Peter is singled out for correction. Why?
Obviously, since Peter was the leader of all,
it was his example that the others were following.
Whenever a leader misbehaved, Paul felt bound to correct him,
even calling the High Priest "a whitewashed wall"! (Ac 23:3)
Nathan had rebuked David for his immoral conduct. (2 Sm 12:9)
Does that mean that Nathan considered David his subordinate?

☆　　☆　　☆

Eventually, Peter went to Rome and became its first bishop.
His first letter was written from Rome (1 Pt 5:13):
"The Church of Babylon (= Rome; cf Rev 17:5,9) salutes you."
He was crucified head-down and buried on the Vatican hill.
The 263 men who succeeded him as the bishop of Rome
have claimed to teach with the authority of Christ Himself:

"Simon, feed my lambs . . . Be shepherd to my sheep."
In his book *Against Heresies* (180 A.D.)
St. Ireneus makes a significant observation
on the importance of oral tradition,
handed on by the Apostles to their successors, the bishops.
To be assured that any given doctrine is sound,
one has only to trace the line of bishops in his community
back to the preaching of an Apostle.
"But since it would take too long in a work of this nature
to enumerate the succession (of bishops) in all the churches,
(we shall limit ourselves) to that of the greatest
and oldest and best known Church of all,
founded and established at Rome
by the two most glorious apostles Peter and Paul . . .
For with this Church, *because of its greater preeminence,*
every other church throughout the world
must bring itself into conformity;
for in this Church
the tradition which has come down from the apostles
has always been preserved . . ." (*Adv. Haer.* 3:3:2)

50

Jerusalem, three weeks later. JESUS crosses the Kedron Valley with the ELEVEN. They begin the ascent of the Mount of Olives.

Acts 1:1-11 / Jn 15:26 / Mt 28:16-20

JESUS   When you return to Jerusalem,
you must wait for the coming of the Holy Spirit.
I will send him to you from the Father,
the Spirit of truth, who will teach you everything.
John baptized with water,
but in a few days,
you will be baptized with the Holy Spirit.

JAMES   Lord, does that mean you will free us from Rome
and restore our former kingdom?

JESUS   The future is not yours to know —
it remains in the hands of my Father.
But when the Holy Spirit has come upon you,
you will be filled with power
to be my witnesses in Jerusalem, Judea, Samaria,
and even to the ends of the earth.

(They reach the top of the mount. JESUS turns to face them. With arms extended, he continues.)

I have been given all power in heaven and on earth.
Go, make all the peoples of the world my followers.
Baptize them in the name of the Father,
and of the Son, and of the Holy Spirit.
Teach them to observe all that I commanded you.
And remember I am with you all days,
even to the end of the world!

JESUS *is lifted up and disappears in a cloud.*
Enter TWO ANGELS *dressed in white.*

202

ANGEL   Men of Galilee!
Why are you standing there staring at the sky?
Jesus has returned to heaven.
You saw him leave on the clouds of heaven —
and he shall return in the same way.

☆   ☆   ☆

CHORUS   *Then I, Daniel, gazed into the vision of the night*
and I saw someone like a Son of Man
coming on the clouds of heaven.
He drew near to the Eternal One
and was presented to Him.
He was given a kingdom and power and glory.
All the nations of the earth became his subjects.
His power is an everlasting power —
and his kingdom will never come to an end.
                        — Daniel 7:13,14

THREE IN ONE

Where does the word "Trinity" occur in the Bible?
You will search in vain, for the word does not appear,
but the reality behind that technical term does.
For by the mystery of the Trinity is meant:
In one and the same God, there are three divine Persons.
Or stated more clearly:
There are three Persons who are completely God.
Each Person is completely separate from the other.
There are not three Gods but only ONE!
It is a mystery, for it surpasses our human understanding.
Yet Jesus revealed it, so we must accept it.
He Himself claimed to be one with the Godhead:
"The Father and I (*two persons*) are one (*being*)." (Jn 10:30)
In the final commission to His disciples (Mt 28:19),
He told them to baptize "in the name
of the Father and of the Son and of the Holy Spirit."
It would be irrational to link unequals with equals.
How would you react to someone who said:
"I would like you to meet three of my friends:
Donna, Mary, and Joan's foot."

But it is inconceivable that Jesus was irrational!
Therefore, we must conclude:
When Jesus linked "Father, Son, and Holy Spirit" together,
— since the *Father* is a divine Person —
so are the *Son* and the *Holy Spirit!*
The very last verse of 2nd Corinthians is similar:
(This is one of the opening greetings at Mass.)
"The grace of Our Lord Jesus Christ (= the Son)
the love of God (= the Father)
and the fellowship of the Holy Spirit be with you all."
Notice the position of the Father — in *second* place!
Namely, it makes no difference in which order they occur:
the three Persons are equal!
Also, notice that this verse uses the word "God"
as a synonym for the "Father" — a common N.T. practice.
Jesus Himself pointed out this fact:
"The one who honors me is my *Father* —
the very one you say is your *God*." (Jn 8:54)
Keep this rule in mind as you read the N.T.,
to avoid any possible misunderstandings.
For example, when you read a passage like this:
"God raised this Jesus from the dead . . ." (Ac 2:32),
you may be tempted to conclude:
"Then Jesus isn't God — since God raised him up."
Remember, "God" and "the Father" are often synonyms.
Jesus is not "God the Father";
He *is* "God the Son",
having the same identical divine nature as the Father.
Another trinitarian passage occurs in Galatians 4:4:
"When the proper time came, GOD sent His SON,
born of a woman, born under the Law,
to make us His adopted children.
Then God sent the SPIRIT of His Son into our hearts,
giving us the right to call Him, *Abba, Father!*"
On Pentecost God first poured out the Spirit of His Son
upon the Apostles in the form of tongues of fire. (Ac 2:4)
They went forth from that upper room,
filled with power and courage,
to spread the message of Jesus to the ends of the globe.

Almost two thousand years have passed since then,
yet the message continues to live;
for we are the results of their labors.
But we cannot hide the precious gift we have received:
"You are the light of the world!
Let your light shine before men
so that they may see your good works
and praise your Father in heaven." (Mt 5:14-16)
Jesus has preceded us to heaven
to prepare a place for us. (Jn 14:2)
"Eye has not seen,
ear has not heard,
nor has the heart of man ever experienced
what God has prepared for those who love Him." (1 Co 2:9)
After a life spent in knowing, loving, and serving God,
may we finally hear that blessed summons:
"Well done, good and faithful servant!
Because you have been faithful over a few things,
I will place you over many things.
Enter into the joy of your Lord!" (Mt 25:21)

EPILOGUE

Almost twenty centuries ago
there was a Man born contrary to the laws of life . . .
He lived in poverty;
He possessed neither wealth nor social prestige.
In infancy He startled a king;
in childhood He puzzled doctors;
in manhood He ruled the course of nature,
walked upon the billows as pavements,
and hushed the sea to sleep.
He had no cornfields or fisheries,
but He could spread a table for five thousand
and have bread and fish to spare.
He healed the multitudes without medicine
and made no charge for His service.
He never wrote a book,
and yet all the libraries of the country
could not hold the books that have been written about Him.
He never wrote a song,
and yet He has furnished the theme for more songs
than all the songwriters combined.
He never founded a college,
but all the schools put together
cannot boast of having as many students.
He never marshaled an army,
nor drafted a soldier,
nor fired a gun;
and yet no leader ever had more volunteers . . .
He never practiced psychiatry,
and yet He has healed more broken hearts
than all the doctors far and near.
When He died few men mourned.
But a black crepe was hung over the sun.
Though men trembled not for their sins,
the earth beneath them shook under the load.
All nature honored Him.
Sinners alone rejected Him.
Corruption could not get hold of His body.

The soil that had been reddened with His blood
could not claim His dust.
Once each week the wheels of commerce cease their turning
and multitudes wend their way to worshipping assemblies
to pay homage and respect to Him.
Like Thomas, could anyone in his right mind
keep from exclaiming:

"MY LORD AND MY GOD!"

Reprinted with the permission of the Servants of the Paraclete, 13270 Maple
Drive, St. Louis, Mo. 63127.